Sherif E. Hegazy

CU00840310

Mr.

ASDA

Contents

Introduction

This is not an autobiography as such, but more an account of some exciting events that took place in my life between 2005 and 2012, in my role as the Marketing and Events Coordinator for ASDA Stafford. I was the head of the local community programme for ASDA in the Stafford region and responsible for the company's Public Relations (PR) in the area, as well as the communications with the press and media.

I have been very privileged to have known so many wonderful and fascinating people, celebrities, and volunteers. I personally knew five Mayors and two MP's in Stafford. I have organized or took part in so many remarkable events. I have enjoyed putting so many smiles on people's and children's faces. I have also enjoyed raising tens of thousands of pounds for various charities and voluntary organizations, some of which I didn't even know existed. It has been a true journey of discovery for me, and for that I am grateful.

Despite the odd hiccup and the usual occupational hazard at times, I almost quit), when I look back now, I realize how lucky I have been and how much I enjoyed the overall experience. That is why I felt it is important to write this book as a recollection of those amazing events and moments. It is as much a reminder for myself as anything. As time goes by, it is easy to forget the details, the names and even the events. Despite my best efforts, the listings here are not by any means comprehensive, it is just the highlights of my experience over the seven years.

Don't get me wrong, this was not plain sailing all the time by any means. As I will explain later, my role was quite new for the company, and the title and description even changed several times in the five years. This meant that the company was experimenting to tweak the role to its current state (which I believe is the optimal). This meant that even some of my managers didn't understand exactly what my role was. With managers changing as often as 12 months in some cases, it was an uphill struggle in some cases to build the trust needed to have the freedom to get on with my role and explore. I had to make it up as I went along, and in many cases improvise. I had to take the initiative and the responsibility to move forward. I was actually writing the job description myself as I went along over the first few years. I created my own job. This might have created friction and clashes, even jealousy and in a couple of cases, even bullying by some managers, sometimes work place politics took over, by people who felt I overstepped my limit. In my defence, I always took great pride in my job, and strived to be the best. I loved the challenge and felt I was on top of the world and that I made a real difference.

I felt I needed to share my journey and I hope this book will be an inspiration and motivation to the reader. But at the same time, I hope it is an enjoyable reading for any one. I don't wish to change any perceptions or ideas, or promote ASDA itself, as this is not a promotion in any way, but I will say this: for many people, ASDA will not be just a supermarket ever again! I am not trying to glorify or slander ASDA, I am grateful for the opportunity it gave me and the chance to learn and explore and be creative. As in any large corporation, there are always drawbacks and advantages, and it is not the aim of this book is not to explore those. My aim is to list some fascinating events that I was lucky enough to be involved in. In doing so, I hope I shed some light on the amazing work so many charities and voluntary organizations do. I hope this will inspire some readers to go out there, explore what they have in their local communities, engage with it and may be even get involved in. It is an extremely rewarding experience.

Finally, I hope you enjoy reading this book, and find it not just amusing but informative. I made good decisions, bad decisions and all in between. At the end, it worked out well, and all I can say is that I did my way...

Sherif E. Hegazy

Stafford, UK, 2012

Chapter One

The Beginning...

It all started in August 2004. I had just moved to Stafford and I was looking for a part time job while finishing my PhD, just to help with day to day expenses and earn some extra money. I didn't know a single person in Stafford. I had a couple of very nice Spanish neighbours, and they took me on my first trip to ASDA Stafford! An interesting experience. I was quite disorientated and all I remember is their Ford KA driving into the ASDA Stafford car park. Lots of cars, trolleys, and grey. Lots of glass buildings. It felt like an island. It was very different from the town, and quite a bit away too. I can't remember the contents of my first shopping basket.

When we came back, I mentioned that I was looking for job. Alan, the Spanish guy said:" Try ASDA! They recruit a lot of part time jobs." I didn't take it seriously, as I was not very keen, or may be a bit intimidated by the big corporation supermarket. I felt it was a responsibility to work for a big company like that, and at that time, I just didn't need any extra worry. A week later, Alan asked me if I applied, and I guess I felt guilty or disrespectful not to have taken his advice so l went and got an application form. The application form was very long. It was very colourful though, which made it easier to fill all your life history! I handed in my application form, and didn't think I would get a job, but the competitive spirit in me hoped I would not be rejected. It would be a blow to my ego I suppose.

Four weeks later, I got a phone call from ASDA, and guess what: I was invited for an interview. The way it works in ASDA, you get invited to a group interview, with 15 to 20 people, and then a selection process takes place. A week later you get a personal interview if you pass the group one. One of the tasks in the group interview is team work. We were divided into teams of four or five people, and our task was to design an advert for ASDA. This included the wording and an illustration. I remember clearly that I had an idea, and we developed it and I presented. I think we did very well! The idea was to change the Old McDonald had a farm song, into that Old McDonald sold his farm because now he's got the ASDA farm (i.e.; he can get all his needs from ASDA). I drew a cute illustration of the farm, ASDA and some animals and products. I think we did well, and I was invited to one-to-one interview. My interview was with Wendy Bobela, the Check outs manager at that time, who was a lovely lady. She was very calm and accommodating, and I had no more worries or anxieties about the job after the interview. The rest will be history after you read this book!

My first job was as check out operator. We had two weeks of training, including the Health and Safety, Happy to Help and much more. At the end, I had only two hours on the actual check out and then was serving customer life!! That was a bit of a shock, but I had a training buddy, who helped me with codes and the many different operations you need to know about (e.g.; payment methods, cash, cheque, or card). After the first week, I was doing quite well, and it became a routine.

I met many interesting customers, chatted about the weather, the weekend, the PhD, cars, music and everything else. I had a few nasty customers too. I still remember many of them and they always say hello (I mean the nice ones!).

I remember working 12 hour shifts in order to reduce the number of days I worked. I needed to leave time for my PhD studies. These shifts were long, and at times slow and boring. But all the staff or Colleagues as we call them at ASDA were very friendly and helpful, and that kept me going. I took pride in my job and strived to do my best. I felt the company entrusted me with the front line service, so I had to do my best.

After a few month, the monotonous job became too much, and I reduced my hours and was seriously considering leaving. I don't cope very well with repetitive tasks, and much prefer a challenge. I then noticed an internal job ad on the board for an Events Coordinator. I had no clue what that is, so I asked one of my manager, Karen Gask, who was a lovely lady and had helped me a lot through the years. She said it is just organizing in-store events and promotions. I still didn't know what it was exactly, but I felt this could be the opportunity for a new challenge. Besides, I had nothing to lose. As I realized later, many in store managers didn't know either. There was no specific job description. So, I filled in an application form and handed it in. I listed everything I can do, all the languages I speak (five), and any other skills I had. Then, there was an interview. Apparently more people applied to the job, but I never got to know who. May be I didn't care at that time.

For the interview, I was asked to prepare some ideas and a plan of action for an upcoming event: The Tickled Pink Breast Cancer research campaign that ASDA supports nationally every year. That was a daunting task for me. The campaign was in its eighth year, and so much has been done before, I had no experience. I thought to myself: This is it. I have no chance. But the fighter in me refused to give up and I decided to give my best shot. I didn't even think about what I was going to do if I didn't get the job. Will I leave? Will I continue on the checkouts? My only goal was to get that job. Even though, I didn't know what it exactly was (and as I realized much later, nor did most of the managers!).

On the day of the interview, in August 2005, I put a tie on, a white shirt and prepared a presentation on the event. I remember very well: I was very nervous. The presentation went well, in front of Karen Gask, my manager, and Francis Raynes, our General Store Manager (GSM). I remember how I divided the store into three areas: Car park,

11

Foyer and Checkouts. I presumed these will be the key areas we need to target for a successful event. The GSM later praised my presentation and my classification. Later that day I got a phone call from Karen, congratulating me and asking me to start straight away, as we only had two weeks to prepare for the Tickled Pink event, which will be my first successful event.

I was over the moon! I made it! I proved to myself that I can do it! I can now go to work proud of my achievement and new position. I celebrated, but was also aware of the responsibility and the trust invested in me, and I don't like to let people down. I vowed to do my best.

My first event, was Tickled Pink fundraiser, in Sept. 2005. I had great support from Karen Gask and Wendy Bobela. I arranged for a raffle to win a ride in a Pink Limo, the limo was on display at the front of the store, we had face painting in the Foyer of the store, many colleagues and managers dressed up, I hired the fancy dress costumes (and bargained for a discount!), I wrote my first press release and we had coverage in all the local press, I was interviewed on Radio Stoke (I had to get up 6:00am to be online for the Breakfast show. I didn't mind, as I didn't sleep much that day anyway because of excitement and anxiety!). We had loads of pink balloons.

I pulled it off. The event was a major success, raised over £800, and I served my apprenticeship!! Of all the events I organized since, this must be the closest to my heart. It really changed my life, and the next five years.

Many events followed, I list some of the highlights later, but what I learned from the first one was invaluable. I learned how to organize people, arrange tasks, speak publicly, approach the public, the media and the press, and most of all, have the confidence to do things I never did before.

Settling In

Shortly after my first successful event, I began to feel my way around my new job. My job description changed, so did my location in the Store. I have now moved from checkouts to the upper floor, were all the offices are, and all the managers sit. I had a mobile phone and got my own login onto the Wal-Mart internal network (WIRE). It connects all ASDA stores and depots in the UK, and is directly link to Wal-Mart in the USA.

Wal-Mart introduced a very structured system for all managers to work in. The WIRE contains daily, weekly and quarterly briefs, telling each manager what to do each day. They also get a check list to tick, for internal audits. All the information is feed through instantly to the head office. All orders, stock, pricing and withdrawals are processed almost real time. So at any time, a manager can check the current stock on the shop floor, re-order or verify deliveries. The warehouse itself was very organized and each store has a modest warehouse, as size doesn't matter. Products need to be on the shelves not stocked in a warehouse. It is all about sales. There are several large Depots across the UK, and these are the big warehouses where the deliveries usually come from in the green ASDA trucks.

But even those are just transient. ASDA took Wal-Mart's strategy not to store any product longer than it takes to deliver and distribute. This makes sense and makes the whole process more efficient and cost effective. Storage and time mean money. In some products, this is a must, such as fresh produce. In other cases it is simply too expensive, such as keeping the freezers running. All this require a robust distribution network and logistics department.

In fact, Wal-Mart in the US doesn't pay for any product till it has actually gone through the till and paid for by the customer. That is how efficient their network is, how strong the reputation of the brand. So in effect, Wal-Mart acts as a broker.

Anyway, I had my user name and password, I had my internal Wal-Mart email address and it felt good. I felt I had an important job, but I also felt the responsibility of being an Ambassador for ASDA in the community.

Wal-Mart was also behind the introduction of my job. They are very conscious of their moral obligation to the community, especially after many years of bad press, and criticism as a ruthless company. So ASDA introduced the Events Coordinator job (which later became local Marketing and Community Officer). As there was no specific job description in the early days as I mentioned earlier; I decided to take it upon myself and improvise. I felt this is a very important job: It affects how people perceive ASDA locally, and no national campaign can replace that. I felt that I was ASDA's representative in the local community (I was representing the ASDA charity foundation later). I went out and reached for charities, local voluntary organizations, schools and council. I tried to find potential cooperation opportunities, and ways in which we at ASDA could help them. From simply promoting their work in the Foyer of the shop, using information stands, to collections or funding, to sponsorship of local charity events. I was also responsible for preparing the bids to the ASDA Foundation to get lottery funding for larger projects (up t0 £50,000), and I was successful in sensing which projects would appeal to the foundation. We raised over £50,000 that way, through grants, matching funding and direct applications.

Next, a few months after I took on my new role, the name changed from Events Coordinator to Marketing Coordinator.

The company realized how important events and promotions in store are, for indirect marketing that they changed the name. I got a digital camera, a photo printer and other tools of the trade! I was excited about my new role and felt the name sounded good, so I printed my own business cards. I saw the design on one of the cards at the head office and copied it. This felt good! I was somebody now! It turned out, that printing those cards was one of the best moves I made, and I reprinted several times. A business card makes a huge difference in people's perception. It did open a lot of doors and makes it easier for people to remember you. It also makes you look professional and gives you authority.

Four month after the new job, it was Jan. 2006, and it was time for the YBM. The Year Beginning Meeting at ASDA Head Office in Leeds is a major annual event. Several delegates from managers, depots and stores meet and lay out the plan for next year. It is also a big celebration and a thank you to everyone for last year's achievements. All ASDA employees are called colleagues, which I suppose stems from Wal-Mart's associates. It does have a warm sound to it, like friends or pals, but after a while it gets to you!

The YBM was a great event. The company hired me a brand new car to go to Leeds (about 3 hours drive). We stayed at Jurry's Inn, a lovely hotel right in the centre of Leeds. The event was divided into two parts: The first part was the conference, that was between 10:00am and 4:00pm, then there was the evening party. Both took place in the historical Town Hall in Leeds, a truly great venue! In total, there were over 400 delegates.

In the conference, awards were given out to the best events coordinators, those who achieved full accreditation (i.e.: completed all their events on time). I was in the job for only four months, so didn't qualify, but this lovely event has motivated me and made me determined to get an award next year. This was not to be, as the conference was cancelled the year after due to cost cutting and sponsors like Persil pulling out.

After the conference, I started to get into my job. I became more organized, started to gather more local contacts, including the Mayor, the local MP, and the hospital. My first Mayoral visit took place in 2006, for an army collection in store. I then visited the Council Buildings for the first time, to complete paper work related to the Mayor's visit. That was when I met Mrs. June Kelleghan, the Mayor's secretary, a lovely lady who became a good friend and later introduced me to the Rotary Club of Stafford Knot. She also was the president of the club for year.

I tried to attend all important events in the Stafford social such as the Mayor's Ball, in order to meet as many people as I could.

I started to write my own press releases, as I had more events than the ones we had to do get accreditation (there are corporate events that had to be organized, but we had the freedom to organize more events that are relevant to the local community, an area which I enjoyed much more). I got to know the editors of the local newspaper, and began to get a sense for a good story and a good event that would be most likely to be published by the paper and at the same time would be good for the local community.

Stop, Look and Listen

One thing I learned very quickly: open your eyes, stop, look and listen. Ideas for events come from people and local community. At first I struggled to find ideas for events, and organizing interesting fundraisers or events that would be interesting to the public, beneficial to ASDA, and would make a good story. That was not easy.

After a while, I was becoming well known in Stafford, because of my pictures in the local papers and the publicity of what I did in the local community. People started to approach me, asking for raffle prizes, support, charity collections, etc. I quickly spotted the opportunity and the potential: these were causes ready to be helped, and people needed them. With a little tweaking and some razzmatazz, a simple collection or fundraiser could be turned into a full blown event. That was my Eureka moment. Helping people and charities make their events and collections more fun and exciting. It worked well for all of us; the collections went well, and with an average 8000 footfall in the store daily, some raised over £1000 per day. For ASDA, we had excellent press coverage and the newspaper loved the costumes and decorations I put on. The foyer was buzzing with activity almost every weekend, with people dressed up, music, and even dancing. I will cover some of these events in the next few chapters.

The bottom line was: I realized that my talent was in turning a simple event into a ball! We had an article in the newspapers almost every week, we had excellent feedback from the public, and I felt I was making a real difference. We raised over £100,000 for local and national charities.

Another part of my role is to represent the ASDA Charity Foundation, which sponsors local worthwhile projects, charities, schools and other community initiatives. I enjoyed that and we had great success in sponsoring over £40,000 worth of projects.

Over the next five years, I generated over 200 articles and photographs in the local newspapers, with several front page stories and everyone in Stafford knew me, and I knew everybody who was anybody. I became a familiar face in the local papers, and members of the public recognized me on the street. Though many didn't remember my name, to them I was the man from ASDA who does all these good deeds in the paper!

I took great pride in my job, and took it very seriously indeed. I felt that I could help local organizations and charities, not just in terms of fundraising, but in terms of raising their profile. I used my connections to get good coverage for various charities and school, to get them out there and make them known to the public. I felt that this could be more valuable than money. And it was indeed. I had so many thank you letters from local charities organizations and individuals whom I helped or got in the papers through an event or fundraiser. I considered myself the middleman, and used my role at ASDA for a good cause. It was a great feeling.

In one instance, I even started a campaign at a local School, Marshlands, to protest against funding cuts, and organized the parents. I created a story that the local press soon sympathised with, and reacted to. We had great coverage and later on the cut plans were axed.

I became a governor at the Marshlands Special school, in Wildwood in Stafford in 2006, after a successful project we sponsored through the ASDA Foundation to transform their sensory garden, I also got involved myself and organized a group of volunteers to do the work. The Mayor and the local Member of Parliament opened the garden.

I joined the Rotary Club of Stafford castle in 2009, through my good friend Cllr Ann Edgeller, the ex-Mayor of Stafford. Through that, I met many of the elite in Stafford, many decent people. Some of them were famous architects, others famous estate agents, lawyers accountants, too many to list. I also joined the Friends of Staffordshire's Young Musicians (FOSYM), a charity that supports young musicians. I became the Treasurer in 2009 and designed their website. I was also a member of the Town Centre Partnership. In June 2009, after being involved in the local elections, I joined the conservative Association. I also joined the Polish White Eagle Club in Stafford after working on a project with them.

When I walked in the Stafford town centre, many people recognized me on the street from the photos in the newspapers, or through events in the store in ASDA. Young children recognized my in queues in banks or in shops and I could hear them tell their parent: the man from ASDA, he painted my face, he gave me the free book, a chocolate, etc. It was a lovely feeling. One day when I went to the HSBC Bank, the lady at the counter, couldn't remember my name, but said she sees me in the newspaper often and she called me: Mr. ASDA! That name stayed with me for a while, and it best describes how popular our activities were, and how people affectionately recognized me. Many times in the street people I never met before stopped me and thanked me for all the good work I do for charity. This meant the world to me and made it all worthwhile.

I became a local celebrity for the right reasons. I enjoyed helping people and making a real difference.

In November 2009, the local Express & Star newspaper ran a full page story about me and my charity and community work in their weekly edition, with five photos of myself at different events. It was a lovely surprise, especially when I was told by the reporter that the Staff at the paper recommended me for the feature on local heroes, because of all the good work I did in the local community.

In 2008, in the St. John Ambulance Annual Pre-Conference meeting and assembly at the lovely county buildings in Stafford (looks like the Houses of Parliament with a big dome and a senate room); the Commander of Staffordshire and the Grand Prior of St. John in England and the Islands awarded me the St. John Order Cross for my services to St. John Ambulance in Staffordshire. It was a great honour. I wear the cross with great pride. That was another proud moment in my career. I was later told by one member of the St. John Priory in London that only five such awards were granted in the past ten years.

In the general elections in May 2010, I was even approached by several people to stand as an Independent Parliamentary candidate.

By now, I was invited to the major events on the Stafford local social and political scene, from the annual Mayor's making, Mayor's Ball to the local Theatre Gala opening nights.

When I look back now, I know I achieved so much and I am proud of it. To some people, this job was dressing up, looking funny and being a clown to entertain the shoppers at ASDA. Before I took it on, it was vacant for 12 months. Well, the clown turned important and I had more influence and impact in Stafford than many politicians. More people in Stafford knew who I was than they knew who the local MP or Mayor was. But most of all, I was proud I used my popularity for a good cause and helped many local voluntary and charity organizations.

PR Guru

By 2007, I had perfected my style in writing press releases that wet the editors' appetites, and knew much of the important information needed to create good coverage for an event. No matter how small or insignificant an event was, I managed to turn it into a festival. Even if at least in the press release I wrote. The timing of the events was important. You need to get in before the cut off date for the print of the next issue of the paper. The press release itself needs to be sent at least three days before the actual event to ensure an entry in the newspapers photographer's diary. Sometimes, it is important to make the call, and speak personally to the reporters to sell the event.

A photo is better than a 1000 words. That is something I totally believe in. I like photography myself; it is a hobby of mine. Sometimes newspapers are short on photographers or use free lance. So, after learning the formats each newspaper prefers (some like group photos, some like portrait with less people, some like children in the picture, some don't like cheque presentation); I started to stage my own photos, using my modest Kodak point and shoot digital camera. My photographers were usually the porters in ASDA, or the Greeter at the door. In some cases, I even asked passersby, after staging the set and showing them the right angle. I always took several shots in different poses and different light conditions then went back home and processed them.

Many times on my break in ASDA, I used to go to our quite room, where we had a little library of old book that colleagues used to bring in, and I would go through photography books, to learn more about composition, colour, lenses and anything I could about taking a good photo.

Colour coordination in a photo is important: A colourful and funny photo is more likely to appeal to the papers and be published. So a funny pose, pink hair or an orange jacket, a costume are all good! A Simpsons' tie is useful for a school visit, a music tie for the music festival.

As a result, I managed to increase the coverage, and provided the papers with the story, and the photo, all by email, so they are ready to be inserted in the paper. That was another thing I learned: Technology. Editors prefer an email to a fax. It is much easier to use the electronic version rather than retyping the fax. I used to rush back home after each event, as we didn't have an internet connection or the software at ASDA; to download the photos from my memory card, pick the best one, improve it and then send it to the papers as fresh as possible. If you wait, then it is not news! In most cases, the papers got the story and the photos within a couple of hours. That was faster than their own photographers. In many cases, my press releases were directly used as they are in my own words.

I believe that a story in the paper should be interesting for the reader and should not be plain advertising for ASDA. So, in all of my press releases, the main story was not about ASDA. It was about a local event, a local charity or a local person. In short, I made ASDA a supporting act for the main event, even though in many cases I organized the event and put it together. This way, newspapers didn't feel compromised by publishing the story, as the business is not the main theme, and it is not direct advertising. At the same time, the story was interesting for local readers, as it is not just praising ASDA all the time!

At times, I had two stories per week, both good. I have a massive library of photos, and I began to archive and catalogue them.

All the hard work paid off: In 2007 I won my first national award: The best local PR among over 400 ASDA stores in the UK (national Gold PR award). I travelled to ASDA Head office in Leeds, and the company hired me a new car to receive the Gold award. It was one of the greatest days in my life. I couldn't believe it when the Store manager informed me. I didn't know what to do!

It was my first visit to the head office, ASDA House in Leeds. An interesting open plan office building that looks more like a shopping mall. There I met the PR Team, along with the lady I was in contact all this time, and finally put a face to the name. She was Rebecca Liburd, head of PR. I sent her my press cuttings every quarter, in my own format to make them look like professional ASDA publication. She praised my packs and reports, and I was pleased to find out that she was actually showing them to all her colleagues.

I received the award from David Smith, the People Director at ASDA. I got my certificate and listened to the praise to my work. I was the proudest man in the world. I knew that that is what I want to do: PR.

Other people I met in ASDA management over the years include Andy Bond, ASDA CEO (2005-2010), Doug Gurr, VP and Director of Logistics, a true legend.

Another important name, at least to me was Julie Ward, the manager of the ASDA Foundation, who has supported and trusted me with various grants over the years, and we created many success stories, through local community projects.

I won the national Gold PR award again in 2008 and 2009, among 300 stores and regions. I also won the Gold community for the best community involvement, and the Gold award for the In-store events. In 2010 and 2011, I was selected to be one of the Faces of ASDA in the National Christmas Ads campaign. I travelled to the Head Office in Leads for the professional photo shoot.

In recognition of the importance of local PR and the local community, in April 2010, ASDA changed the title of my role to Community Officer, which made me feel so proud, that my feedback and my hard work made a difference and the company listened. I always believed in the importance of being involved with the local community, and went the extra mile, outside my job role sometimes and in my own time. The PR initiatives and community events I took on myself were not a requirement of the original role. I pushed myself and created a role within the role, setting my own targets and challenges. I had a vision: to promote the company. I believed in the power of PR. Now my ideas are adapted and they became a requirement. When the GSM (General Store Manager) read the new role description to me, my initial thoughts were: I couldn't have written it better myself, it is as if the role was tailored to me and what I have been doing and fighting for over the past few years!

I always considered myself ASDA's Ambassador in the local community, that was the role I created and pursued; and now after years of success and in recognition of the importance of that role, the company decided to adopt and implement the new role officially based on what I was doing for such a long time singlehanded.

That was a very brief introduction about my career at ASDA in the past five years, and doesn't cover any details or even anywhere near. I just felt I need to explain the beginnings and the fact that I had no training in that job, and how I evolved with it through the years. There were some very bad and upsetting moments in my career, but I prefer to look at the bright side and the final result and achievements.

I would like to think that I used my role in ASDA to make a real difference in the local community, and help as many organizations, community groups and charities as I possibly could. ASDA was a platform to serve the community, I always believed that. And in 2010, the company recognized the importance and impact of the local community to the overall customer perception, and spread the message across the chain about the importance of the local community. I feel that I have contributed in changing the perspective of a community role on so many levels at the ASDA Head office, a fact that I am proud of. Several people at the Head office in Leeds expressed to me personally how much of an impact I made on the role and the local PR strategy.

Well, I guess it is enough about me, and let's move to some of the actual events, which I can proudly and fondly remember over the years. There isn't enough space to list everything I ever did, so I classified the highlights into categories, to make easier and more interesting to read. I have included as many photos as possible, as I think it does it justice to see the colourful events and not just read about them. Personally, when I look at a book in the library, I always prefer books with lots of illustrations and photos, and I did that here. Please note that most of the photos in this book were taken or staged by me, using my simple digital camera.

Some of the Awards I've won: Gold award for Best Events, Best PR in the Company (three times).
Above: receiving my awards from Davis Smith, ASDA's People Director in the HQ , Leeds.
Below: my own designed buiseness card.

24

My first ever Event at ASDA: Tickled Pink,
Breast Cancer Research fundraiser, Sept. 2005.

Express & Star, Wednesday May 19, 2010

Boost in store for young musicians

By Shaun Lintern
stafford@expressandstar.co.uk

A Stafford-based charity that supports young musicians has been given a boost by town supermarket Asda.

The store has donated £200 to the Friends of Staffordshire Young Musicians, which helps them through grants and musical equipment, as well as various school music programmes.

It has been running for over 30 years.

The charity also takes part in organising local and national musical events and supporting the Stafford Music festival and the Gatehouse.

It also organises an annual awards ceremony to recognize bright, outstanding young musicians, who receive financial awards and certificates.

The charity relies totally on volunteers, and various fundraising events and grants.

The charity is seeking to connect with more people and a younger generation, through a new look website and update to its profile.

Support

Now, the Asda Foundation has donated £200 to the charity to support the development of the new website, and other services of the charity.

Sherif Hegazy, Asda Foundation representative in Stafford, said: "The Friends of Staffordshire Young Musicians do a lot for young musicians in and around Stafford.

"We we need to let more people know about it and engage more young people into its activities.

"That is why the website is a vital service for the charity. The charity provides excellent services to musicians and schools in Staffordshire and we are proud to be supporting youth and music through the charity."

Friends of Staffordshire Young Musicians have received a donation from Asda in Stafford. Left is Stuart Reynolds, chairman of the charity, with Sherif Hegazy from Asda

One of many newspaper articles about my work in the community. I wrote the press releases, created the stories and arranged the photo calls. In many cases, I staged the photos too. People recognized me on the streets.

Mr. ASDA!! In front of an ASDA lorry at the Stafford store

www.staffordshirenewsletter.co.uk   Staffordshire Newsletter, Thursday, December 30, 2010

NATIONAL HONOURS ... Asda community chief Sherif Hegazy

FACING UP TO ROLE
STAFFORD WORKER'S POSTER CAMPAIGN

A STAFFORD supermarket worker has been chosen as the national face of Asda after a campaign of tireless community work.

Sherif Hegazy, marketing and community officer for Asda's Stafford store, will appear on posters in more than 350 branches across the country.

The 32-year-old Stafford resident has won awards for community involvement and arranging promotional events.

He said: "It was a fantastic surprise and the best Christmas present ever, a fantastic way to end 2010.

"I was informed I'd been chosen along with four other colleagues from different Asda Stores to represent Asda during the Christmas campaign in 2010.

"We had a two-day professional photo shoot at the Asda head office in Leeds, complete with make-up artists. We felt like movie stars."

I was one of only four colleagues out of 150,000 to be featured on the ASDA National Christmas Poster campaign. The posters were displayed at Every ASDA in the UK (350+ stores).

27

Express & Star, Wednesday December 8, 2010

Sherif faces up to national recognition

Posters at every Asda in country

A Stafford man is to have his face on display on the wall of every Asda branch across the country.

Sherif Hegazy, Asda Stafford's marketing and community co-ordinator, has been chosen, along with three other of the company's workers, to be the Face of Asda for a Christmas advertising campaign.

Mr Hegazy said: "It was a fantastic surprise and the best Christmas present ever – a great honour.

"We had a two-day professional photo shoot at the Asda head office in Leeds, complete with make up artists. We felt like movie stars."

Selected

Mr Hegazy, and the three others, were selected over 150,000 colleagues who work in the company's 350 plus stores to front the campaign.

He said he was selected because the Stafford branch has been nationally recognised for positive community work.

He said: "We have raised over £100,000 in the past five years for local causes and charities.

"We also completed several local community projects and work closely with schools. We are very proud of our achievements here in Stafford."

The giant posters are now featured in every Asda store at the customer service desk.

They will remain there throughout the Christmas period.

Sherif Hegazy, from Stafford, will have his picture on display in every Asda store

Proudly holding my Poster, before it was put on display at Stafford ASDA!

Chapter Two

The Green Mile

Many people in Britain know ASDA, the green logo, the ads and slogans, "Always low prices", the "pocket tap", "Britain's lowest priced supermarket". But what do we actually know about ASDA as a company? How many ASDA stores are there in the UK? Are there different types of stores? What about store sizes? How much is ASDA worth? What is their turnover?

It is extremely amusing when I used to go to schools, in career fairs, to see the pupils surprised to see me in a suit! I could see their first impressions and surprise: to them jobs at ASDA are confined to shelf stacking or checkouts. This might sound strange, but as a matter of fact, many people don't realize how versatile the ASDA machine is. ASDA as a company employs IT specialists, accountants, Marketing staff, fashion designers, opticians, pharmacists, drivers, mechanics, artists, engineers, architects and many more.

To understand the company, we need to look back at how it all started over 60 years ago.

History

Asda Stores Limited was founded as **Associated Dairies & Farm Stores Limited** in 1949 in Leeds. The adoption of the Asda name occurred in 1965 with the merger of the Asquith chain of three supermarkets and Associated Dairies; Asda is an abbreviation of **As**quith and **Da**iries, often capitalised.[4] For a short time in the 1980s Asda Stores Ltd was a subsidiary of Asda-MFI plc following a merger between the two companies. Other companies in the group were Associated Dairies Limited, the furniture retailer MFI and Allied Carpets. After the sale of MFI and Allied Carpets the company name changed to Asda Group plc. The dairy division was sold in a management buyout and renamed Associated Fresh Foods,[5] meaning that Asda has since had no connection with one of the firms its name was derived from.

With stores mainly based in the North of England, the newly focused food retail group expanded further south in 1989 by buying the large format stores of rival Gateway Superstores for £705 million. This move overstretched the company and it found itself in deep trouble trying to sell too many different products.[6] As a result it was forced to raise money from shareholders in both 1991 and 1993. It revived under the leadership of Archie Norman, who later became a front bench Conservative MP. CEO from 1991, Norman was chairman of the company during the period 1996–99, and replicated the store on the basis of United States retail giant Wal-Mart, even sending protégé Allan Leighton to Bentonville, Arkansas to assess and photograph the systems and marketing which Wal-Mart had deployed.[7]

In 1997, The Spice Girls licensed their name and image to Asda in which they created over 40 different Spice Items for Christmas 1997 developing goods such as party supplies, official merchandise, and even Spice Girl branded kids meals in the stores' restaurants. The Spice Girls earned £1 million for this sponsorship deal.

When Norman left the company to pursue his political career, he was replaced by Leighton. Wal-Mart wanted to enter the UK market so CEO Bob Martin lobbied British Prime Minister Tony Blair on planning issues.[8] Asda, which at the time owned 230 stores and had planned to merge with Kingfisher plc, was purchased by Wal-Mart on 26 July 1999 for £6.7 billion.[2]

After the takeover Asda continued to maintain its headquarters at the then newly opened "Asda House". This building was one of the first of the new large office blocks to open as part of the redevelopment of the huge area south of the River Aire in the city centre of Leeds, in the Holbeck district, West Yorkshire.

In 2005, amid reported concerns within Wal-Mart about a slippage in market share, partially due to a resurgent Sainsbury's, Asda's chief executive, Tony de Nunzio left, and was replaced by Andy Bond. In 2005, Asda expanded into Northern Ireland by purchasing 12 Safeway stores from Morrisons.[9][10]

In November 2008 there were reports that Asda was to buy Irish retailer Dunnes.[11]

In 2009 Wal-Mart 'sold' Asda for £6.9 billion to their Leeds-based investment subsidiary Corinth Services Limited.[12] The deal, which took place in August, was described as part of a "group restructuring" and means Asda remains under the control of the Wal-Mart, since Corinth are themselves a subsidiary of Wal-Mart.[13]

In May 2010, ASDA acquired Swedish retailer chain Netto's stores in the UK for over £700 million, to support its expansion in the south of the UK. It is also said that recent market research recommended that customers choose a store due to convenience rather than just the price. This could partially explain Tesco's huge market share of 30% compared to ASDA's 17%, despite ASDA's price cuts. Tesco has over 2000 stores in the UK, compared to ASDA's 300.

On 11 May 2010 Andy Clarke, a former manager of an ASDA store, who was also the Chief Operating Officer, was appointed as Chief Executive Officer.[14]

Today, an average ASDA store turns over an average of £1 million per week, employs 500 colleagues, and offers over 35,000 different items for sale. ASDA turns over more than £15 Billion per year. The company is valued at £6.7 Billion (2009).

Marketing

Asda is known for memorable famous marketing campaigns. In the "Asda price" campaign,[15] customers tap their trouser pocket twice, producing a 'chinking' sound as the coins that Asda's low prices have supposedly left in their pockets knock together.

The pocket tap ads were launched in 1977 and over the next 30 years a range of celebrities have been "tappers", including Julie Walters,

Michael Owen, sitcom actor Leonard Rossiter and Carry On actress Hattie Jacques.[16] In the late 1980s, prior to the reintroduction of the tap pocket campaign, advertising for Asda had featured the Fairground Attraction song Perfect. In 2004, Sharon Osbourne was selected to be part of a new marketing campaign by Asda; her last advert was aired in August 2005.

In the smiley face "rollback" campaign, also used in Wal-Mart advertisements, a CGI smiley face bounced from price tag to price tag, knocking them down as customers watch. The focus of these campaigns is to portray Asda as the most affordable supermarket in the country, a claim that was challenged by competitors, especially Aldi. In 2006, Asda advertising was themed around singing children and the slogan "More for you for less", and the previous tap of the trouser pocket advertising was reduced to a double-tap on a stylized 'A', still producing the 'chinking' sound. This included an advert during the 2006 FIFA World Cup featuring the England footballer Michael Owen in an advert with the children singing Vindaloo. In 2007, the advertising campaign abandoned the rollback hook in favour of featuring celebrities including Victoria Wood and Paul Whitehouse working as Asda employees.

For Christmas 2007, Asda reintroduced the "That's Asda price" slogan[17] as well as the famous 'jingle' to some of its adverts, this can also be heard on its instore radio station 'Asda FM'.

Starting in 2008, Asda has been returning to its roots and is now re-focusing on price with its new "Why Pay More?" campaign both on TV and in stores. Current Asda TV commercials in April 2009 focus on price comparisons between Asda and its rivals, using information from "MySupermarket" to suggest that Asda is Britain's most affordable supermarket. The music being used in these adverts is the Billy Childish version of the classic *Dad's Army* theme tune. The old Asda jingle is not included in these,[18] but appeared in a 2008 Christmas advert.[19] Asda returned to the traditional pocket tap adverts in March/April 2009, with the slogan "Saving You Money Every Day!"

Asda has been winner of the *The Grocer* magazine "Lowest Price Supermarket" Award for the past 12 years,[20] and uses this to promote itself across the UK. In August 2005, rival supermarket chain Tesco challenged Asda's ability to use the claim that it was the cheapest supermarket in the country, by complaining to the Advertising Standards Agency. The A.S.A upheld the complaint[21] and ordered Asda to stop using it, citing that *The Grocer* magazine survey was based on limited and unrepresentative evidence as it examined the price of just 33 products, and that the survey did not study low-cost supermarkets such as Aldi, and that their price checker, My Supermarket, doesn't include Morrison's, which was mentioned a few times. As a result Asda no longer cites itself as "Officially Britain's lowest priced supermarket", instead using "Winner: Britain's lowest price supermarket award".

Asda Smart Price

Asda Smart Price is a no-frills private label trade name. The equivalents from the three other big supermarkets are Tesco Value, Sainsbury's Basics and Morrison's Bettabuy range.

The Smart Price brand can trace its origins to Asda's Farm Stores brand launched in the mid 1990s, which consisted of products that were offered at a lower price than the equivalent famous name brand product and Asda's own brand equivalent. The Farm Stores brand originally consisted of a small number of food only products, largely frozen such as frozen chips and a small range of ready meals, this range later expanded to include fresh food.

Smart Price products are almost always the lowest price option (known as *Our Lowest Price*) in a product category in Asda stores. Occasionally this difference is only a few pence, however in others it is a marked difference. For example, a box of Smart Price Biological Washing Powder costs 50 pence while the equivalent Asda brand washing powder costs £1.50 and well known name brand alternatives cost from £2 upwards.

The Smart Price label was originally a food only brand, however over the years it has expanded to cover almost every product range in the store, including clothing and furnishings with the George Smart Price brand. Like early generic products in the US some Smart Price products lack what can be thought of as 'frills' in the modern brand name or supermarket own brand, for example the Smart Price toothpaste has an old fashioned screw cap rather than the now more common flip cap and the Smart Price range of crisps come in traditional clear plastic bags rather than the foil bags common to most name brand versions.

George clothing

Asda has its own range of clothing known as **George** which was created in 1990.[28] This is marketed as quality fashion clothing at affordable prices. Wal-Mart also sells the George brand in the United States, Canada and Japan (and in South Korea until Wal-Mart pulled out of that market). This George label was named after George Davies, the founder of Next, who was its original chief designer. He is no longer associated with the brand, although it has aimed to remain true to the high quality, low price business model that he established.

In 2005, Asda stated that the George range was a £1.75 billion business, including sales from Wal-Mart stores in the USA and Germany. Mintel estimate that George is the fourth largest retailer of clothing in the United Kingdom, after Marks & Spencer, the Arcadia Group and Next.[29]

Asda was the first supermarket to stock wedding dresses. Part of the George line, they cost just £60 while adult bridesmaid dresses ranged between £30 and £35, at launch.[30]

Stores

Asda originally had a "simple and fresh" store format, which under Archie Norman's team and the focus on a Wal-Mart style strategy became even more emphasised. The stores are generally white and green, with simplistic layout but built on a Wal-Mart larger footprint format – Asda's average store is almost 20% bigger than its rivals, but stocks 20% fewer lines.

However, the preferred large-format stores have brought problems to Asda's growth beyond its spurts in both the 1990s and immediate post Wal-Mart era. With the UK's tight planning restrictions, the opportunity to increase retail space via new store builds has been limited. Rather than follow rivals Tesco and Sainsbury's into "local" format smaller-footprint stores, Asda has chosen to adapt its format to niche stores to retain longer term growth.

On 16 April 2010, Asda announced plan to open over 100 new non-food stores in companies ambitious five-year plan.[31]

Asda Wal-Mart Supercentres

Following the takeover by Wal-Mart, several "Asda Wal-Mart Supercentres" have been opened, creating some of the largest hypermarkets in the United Kingdom. The first Supercentre opened in Livingston, Scotland in June 2000. The Milton Keynes store is currently the largest Asda Wal-Mart Supercentre by total floor space. The second largest Asda Wal-Mart Supercentre is located in Huyton, Merseyside. There are currently 25 Supercentres in the UK. It is also planned for a Wal-Mart Supercentre in Dundee, Scotland.

Asda Supermarkets

There are presently 346 Asda Supermarkets. In May 2010, Asda announced the purchase of the 193 UK stores of Danish discount retailer Netto in a £778 million deal. The stores will continue to trade as Netto stores until mid-2011, when Asda plans to integrate the stores into its supermarkets division, designated for shops smaller than 25,000 square feet (2,300 m^2).[32]

Asda Living stores

In October 2003 Asda launched a new format called *'Asda Living'*. This is the company's first "general merchandise" store, containing all its non-food ranges including clothing, home electronics, toys, homewares, health, and beauty products. With these stores they have linked up with Compass Group who operates the coffee shop Caffe Ritazza within some of the stores. The first store with this format opened in Walsall, West Midlands, and at the time of writing has been followed by ten further stores.

George clothing stores

In 2004, the George clothing brand was extended to a number of standalone George stores on the high street. In 2008, all George standalone stores were closed due to high rental costs resulting in low profitability. The first George standalone store to open was in Preston.

Asda Essentials

In April 2006, Asda launched a new format called 'Asda Essentials' in a former Co-op store in Northampton, followed by another in Pontefract a month later. This was modelled on the French Leaderprice[dead link] chain, with a smaller floorplate than Asda's mainstream stores. *Essentials* focuses primarily on own-brand products, only stocking branded items that are perceived to be at the "core" of a family's weekly shop. This style of retailing is an attempt to address competition from discount supermarkets such as Aldi, Lidl and Netto. On 6 December 2006 *The Guardian* newspaper reported that further planned store openings were under review following poor sales in the existing outlets. It was also revealed that the range of branded products has been expanded.[33] In early January 2007 it was announced that the initial trial *Essentials* store would close within a month after only 10 months of trading.

Distribution

Asda also has 70 depots all across the UK which distribute across the network of stores. There are depots for chilled foods, clothing and ambient products, such as fizzy drinks and cereals.[35]

Employee relations

Asda has 150,000 employees, whom it refers to as "colleagues" (90,000 part-time, 60,000 full-time). The company has featured prominently in lists of "Best companies to work for", appearing in second place in *The Times* newspaper list for 2005 (although very few, if any, employees at grass-roots level were asked for their opinion).[42] It offers staff a discount of 10% on most items (exceptions include fuel, stamps, lottery, gift cards and tobacco related items).

The Colleague Circle in every store is a group of colleagues, each of whom represents a store department. Usually about 12 people, headed by the People Manager. Their job is to feedback colleagues concerns and requests. It is also a sort of a social committee, that organizes

Christmas parties, colleagues days out, etc. I was on the circle, as the Community member, and my job was to get our colleagues involved in our community work, and getting volunteers to work on our projects.

We also used the funds in the colleague circle to pay for celebration lunches, to recognize outstanding achievers every month. One of my ideas that was implemented was the purchase of a shoe cleaning machine, as I noticed in winter many colleagues have mucky shoes from rain or snow, and it reflects the wrong image to the customers. We also funded a sofa for the colleague rest room, and a flat screen TV.

Awards

- 1997–present — Voted Britain's lowest price supermarket in a survey by Grocer 33 Magazine
- 2001, 2002, 2003 — Voted a top 10 UK employer by the Sunday Times Top 100 Best Employers Survey, although the merit of Asda being awarded such an award is contested by the GMB
- 2002 Nestlé Social Commitment Award, awarded by peers in the food industry
- March 2009 — Voted 'Innovative Employer of the Year' at the Oracle Retail Week Awards[

Wal-Mart

It would be impossible to talk about ASDA without mentioning Wal-Mart. Not just because of the impact Wal-Mart had on ASDA, but because of the fact that Wal-Mart is the world's biggest company, and ASDA is part of it.

Wal-Mart was founded in 1962 in Bentonville, Arkansas, by the Walton family, who now account for five out of the ten richest people on the planet.[3] Its expansion has been phenomenal. A so called 'strategy of consolidation' smashes local small town businesses, often leaving inhabitants without alternative local retailing outlets. In many ways the story of Wal-Mart reads like a textbook case study of how well a company can do in the current global economic system, and how the rest of the world reacts. H. Lee Scott, the company President, was in 2004 named by Vanity Fair magazine as the most powerful person in the world – above Bill Gates and Rupert Murdoch.

Today, Wal-Mart worldwide employs over 2 million employees or associates, with total revenue of over $400 Billion Dollars. But how did it all begin?

History

Sam Walton's original Walton's Five and Dime store in Bentonville, Arkansas, now serving as the Wal-Mart Visitor's Centre.

Sam Walton, a businessman from Arkansas, began his retail career when he started work on June 3, 1940, at a J.C. Penney store in Des Moines, Iowa where he remained for 18 months. In 1945, he met Butler Brothers, a regional retailer that owned a chain of variety stores called Ben Franklin and that offered him one in Newport, Arkansas.[8]

Walton was extremely successful in running the store in Newport, far exceeding expectations.[9] However, when the lease came up for renewal, Walton could neither come to agreement on the existing store's lease renewal nor find a new location in Newport. Instead, he opened a new Ben Franklin franchise in Bentonville, Arkansas, but called it "Walton's Five and Dime." There, he achieved higher sales volume by marking up slightly less than most competitors.[10]

On July 2, 1962, Walton opened the first Wal-Mart Discount City store located at 719 Walnut Ave. in Rogers, Arkansas. The building is now occupied by a hardware store and a pawn shop. Within five years, the company expanded to 24 stores across Arkansas and reached $12.6 million in sales.[11] In 1968, it opened its first stores outside Arkansas, in Sikeston, Missouri and Claremore, Oklahoma.[12]

Incorporation and growth

The company was incorporated as *Wal-Mart Stores, Inc.* on October 31, 1969. In 1970, it opened its home office and first distribution centre in Bentonville, Arkansas. It had 38 stores operating with 1,500 employees and sales of $44.2 million. It began trading stock as a publicly held company on October 1, 1970, and was soon listed on the New York Stock Exchange. The first stock split occurred in May 1971 at a market price of $47. By this time, Wal-Mart was operating in five states: Arkansas, Kansas, Louisiana, Missouri, and Oklahoma; it entered Tennessee in 1973 and Kentucky and Mississippi in 1974. As it moved into Texas in 1975, there were 125 stores with 7,500 employees and total sales of $340.3 million.[12]

In the 1980s, Walmart continued to grow rapidly, and by its 25th anniversary in 1987 there were 1,198 stores with sales of $15.9 billion and 200,000 associates.[12] This year also marked the completion of the company's satellite network, a $24 million investment linking all operating units of the company with its Bentonville office via two-way voice and data transmission and one-way video communication. At the time, it was the largest private satellite network, allowing the corporate office to track inventory and sales and to instantly communicate to stores.[13] In 1988, Sam Walton stepped down as CEO and was replaced by David Glass.[14] Walton remained as Chairman of the Board, and the company also rearranged other people in senior positions.

In 1988, the first *Walmart Supercenter* opened in Washington, Missouri.[15] Thanks to its superstores, it surpassed Toys "R" Us in toy sales in the late 1990s.[16] The company also opened overseas stores, entering South America in 1995 with stores in Argentina and Brazil; and Europe in 1999, buying Asda in the UK for $10 billion.[17]

In 1998, Walmart introduced the "Neighborhood Market" concept with three stores in Arkansas.[18] By 2005, estimates indicate that the company controlled about 20% of the retail grocery and consumables business.[19]

In 2000, H. Lee Scott became President and CEO, and Walmart's sales increased to $165 billion.[20] In 2002, it was listed for the first time as America's largest corporation on the Fortune 500 list, with revenues of $219.8 billion and profits of $6.7 billion. It has remained there every year, except for 2006.[21][22]

In 2005, Walmart had $312.4 billion in sales, more than 6,200 facilities around the world—including 3,800 stores in the United States and 2,800 elsewhere, employing more than 1.6 million "associates" worldwide. Its U.S. presence grew so rapidly that only small pockets of the country remained further than 60 miles (100 km) from the nearest Wal-Mart.[23]

Wal-Mart International

Wal-Mart's international operations currently comprise 4,081 stores and 664,000 workers in 14 countries outside the United States.[55] There are wholly owned operations in Argentina, Brazil, Canada, and the UK. With 2.1 million employees worldwide, the company is the largest private employer in the US and Mexico, and one of the largest in Canada.[56]

Wal-Mart has operated in Canada since its acquisition of 122 stores comprising the Woolco division of Woolworth Canada, Inc in 1994. As of April 2010, it operates 317 locations (including 89 Supercentres) employing 78,138 Canadians, with a local home office in Mississauga, Ontario.[57] Wal-Mart Canada's first three Supercentres (spelled as in Canadian English) opened on November 8, 2006, in Hamilton, London, and Aurora, Ontario.

Sales in 2006 for Wal-Mart's UK subsidiary, Asda (which retains the name it had before acquisition by Wal-Mart), accounted for 42.7% of sales of Wal-Mart's international division. In contrast to Wal-Mart's US operations, Asda was originally and still remains primarily a grocery chain, but with a stronger focus on non-food items than most UK supermarket chains other than Tesco. At the end of 2007, Asda had 340 stores, some of which are branded Asda Wal-Mart Supercentres, as well as Asda Supermarkets, Asda Living, George High Street and Asda Essentials stores.[58]

In addition to its wholly-owned international operations, Wal-Mart has joint ventures in China and several majority-owned subsidiaries. Wal-Mart's majority-owned subsidiary in Mexico is Walmex. In Japan, Wal-Mart owns about 53% of Seiyu.[59] Additionally, Wal-Mart owns 51% of the Central American Retail Holding Company (CARHCO), consisting of more than 360 supermarkets and other stores in Guatemala, El Salvador, Honduras, Nicaragua, and Costa Rica.[60]

In 2004, Wal-Mart bought the 116 stores in the Bompreço supermarket chain in north-eastern Brazil. In late 2005, it took control of the Brazilian operations of Sonae Distribution Group through its new subsidiary, WMS Supermercados do Brasil, thus acquiring control of the Nacional and Mercadorama supermarket chains, the leaders in the Rio Grande do Sul and Paraná states, respectively. None of these was rebranded. As of April 2010, Wal-Mart operates 64 Super-Bompreço stores, 33 Hyper-Bompreço stores. It also runs 45 Wal-Mart Supercenters, 24 Sam's Club stores, and 101 Todo Dia stores. With the acquisition of Bompreço and Sonae, Wal-Mart is currently the third largest supermarket chain in Brazil, behind Carrefour and Pão de Açúcar.[61]

In June 2006, Wal-Mart was excluded from the investment portfolio of The Government Pension Fund of Norway, which held stock values of about US$ 430 million in the company, due to a social audit into alleged labour rights violations in the company's operations in the US and worldwide.[62][63] Although Wal-Mart did not respond to questions from the fund's auditors, the company later claimed the decision "don't appear to be based on complete information".[64]

In July 2006, Wal-Mart announced its withdrawal from Germany due to sustained losses in a highly competitive market. The stores were sold to the German company Metro during Wal-Mart's fiscal third quarter.[59][65]

In November 2006, Wal-Mart announced a joint venture with Bharti Enterprises to open retail stores in India. As foreign corporations are not allowed to directly enter the retail sector in India, Wal-Mart will operate through franchises and handle the wholesale end.[66] The partnership will involve two joint ventures; Bharti will manage the front end involving opening of retail outlets, while Wal-Mart will take care of the back end, such as cold chains and logistics.

In 2008, Wal-Mart named German retailing veteran Stephan Fanderl as the president of Wal-Mart Emerging Markets-East in an effort to, "explore retail business opportunities in Russia and neighbouring markets." The market is estimated to be worth more than $140 billion per year in food sales alone.[67]

In January 2009, the company acquired a controlling interest in the largest grocer in Chile, Distribucion y Servicio D&S SA.[68]

In February 2010, the company agreed to buy Vudu, a Silicon Valley start-up whose three-year-old online movie service is being built into an increasing number of televisions and Blu-ray players. Terms of the acquisition were not disclosed, but a person briefed on the deal said the price for the company, which raised $60 million in capital, was over $100 million.[69]

Wal-Mart Facts

Type	Public (NYSE: WMT)
Industry	Retailing
Founded	Rogers, Arkansas, U.S. (1962)
Founder(s)	Sam Walton
Headquarters	Bentonville, Arkansas, U.S. Latin American headquarters: Miami, Florida, U.S.[1]
Area served	Worldwide
Key people	Mike Duke (CEO) H. Lee Scott (Chairman of the Executive Committee of the Board) S. Robson Walton (Chairman)
Products	Discount Stores Supercenters Neighbourhood Markets
Revenue	▲ US$ 408.21 billion (2009)[2]
Operating	▲ US$ 23.95 billion (2009)[3]

income

Net income	▲ US$ 14.33 billion (2009)[3]
Total assets	▼ US$ 170.70 billion (2010)[4]
Total equity	▲ US$ 70.74 billion (2009)[3]
Employees	approx. 2,100,000 (2009)[5]
Website	www.walmartstores.com www.walmart.com

Source: Wikipedia.org, 2010

ASDA and Wal-Mart

As mentioned before, in 1999 ASDA became wholly owned by Wal-Mart Inc. It was an important move for Wal-Mart to get into the European market. Wal-Mart's international division contributes 18% to their total sales, with ASDA accounting for nearly half of that.[8]

The acquisition by Wal-Mart greatly helped ASDA's logistic operations, with the new in house automated systems, as well the internal structure of the operations. ASDA's internal network is actually a replica of Wal-Mart's and is connected to it. As a matter of fact, every Wal-Mart owned store around the world is connected to US, and live video conferencing facilities as well as stock control systems are all in place.

Every product sold through the tills at ASDA is immediately reflected in the depot, warehouse and stock. Automatic re-ordering and re-stocking levels are maintained through the system. At any 24 hour period, the head office can see a live image of the situation of sales, warehouse stock, sales statistics, customer numbers and average spend. A sophisticated suit of IT software is maintained in house by ASDA and Wal-Mart to support the complicated real-time support network.

The internal network is actually called the WIRE (Wal-Mart Integrated Retail Environment).

ASDA's image in the UK though has suffered, due to Wal-Mart's reputation as a ruthless retailer. Wal-Mart's employee relations and unethical practices were not that promising for the UK market place. The general prospect of an American company buying out a British retailer was not very welcome.

ASDA worked hard to restore public confidence and took the best of Wal-Mart's experience, which included the open work practices and more focus on the local community. ASDA did not change its name after the takeover, to emphasis its Britishness, and maintain an independent image.

One great idea that came from Wal-Mart and made a huge difference to customer experience and set ASDA apart from its competitors was the Greeter. The Greeter was an ASDA Colleagues who usually stood at the front of the store with a microphone and asset of keys. His or Her job was literary to greet customers as they walk into the store. Occasionally, the Greeter would make an announcement on the internal radio using the microphone about an offer in the store today, or asking for a lost child to come to the front of the store to the parent. He would also tell shoppers about any collections or events happening in the store today.

Another important part of the job would be to give customers the disabled scooters and wheel chairs on request. He would also be watching the entrance and exit, to stop any customers in case of a security tag going off.

Despite the apparent simplicity of the job, I personally had some fantastic feedback from customers, who said that the Greeter made them feel welcome and they had a friendly face to ask for the location of items or any general question or directions. It did set ASDA aside from the competition (other supermarkets didn't have that). In our store, we had lovely Greeters, like Sally Goulder, Tom Hall and Mandy Montgomery. As they worked shifts, there would be a different greeter at different days and times.

All in all, Wal-Mart helped ASDA make its operations more efficient. This reflected on ASDA's market share, which went up to over 17%, and ASDA became the second largest UK retailer after Tesco. This is despite having eight times less outlets than TESCO. This is where the next section comes in. Customer perception of ASDA has been completely transformed into the Giant green responsible retailer, through the massive local community programme campaign, which was part of my job.

ASDA in the Community

In order to improve its image, ASDA decided to give something back, and focus locally. A special division was set up in the early 2000's, first to deliver in-store events and promotions, but then expanded to include the local community. Two new departments in ASDA House were working closely together: PR and Events. It started with a very small budget, and many creative ideas. It was later expanded in 2005, and got more funding and designated colleagues. That was when I joined the team through my Job, the Events Coordinator.

From a tiny £50 per quarter budget, we started created a buzz in stores: dressing up, colouring, improvising, whatever we could do to attract customer attention and be the friendly supermarket!

The focus was to support charities and community initiatives. Originally, we were supporting a couple of national corporate charities, such as Tickled Pink, Breast Cancer research and BBC Children In Need. This was later expanded to include many local charities and good causes, as well as schools, local sports, council and any good cause that could make a difference in the local community, and generate positive PR for ASDA.

The company realized how powerful good local PR was, sometimes called indirect marketing. It was also much cheaper than advertising in local papers. Market research showed that the work we were doing locally generated more business than many expensive ads.

As a result, the ASDA Foundation was born in 2005 and the marketing emphasis shifted towards local PR.

The ASDA Foundation is a charity organization, partly funded by ASDA and partly by lottery grants. The aim is to support worthwhile sustainable projects, that make a difference to the local community.

This was a great initiative. Now, we could fund local projects of up to £50,000. We now had real power to make a real difference in the local community. It was my job to research the projects, prepare estimates and budgets and put applications forward.

In Stafford, we had some great success stories, including a children's playground, a sensory garden for special school, a WWII memorial, disabled facilities in a social club and a Guinness record attempt just to mention a few.

Julie Ward was the Manager of the foundation between 2005 and 2010, and she is a good friend of mine. She is a lovely person, and she trusted me with the work. She would recommend the projects to the trustees, who then decide on which projects to go for from all the applications from around the UK. The Foundation had control of over £2 million in funds.

Wal-Mart was also behind the push towards community and social responsibility, and we had to submit detailed account of our community hours, cash raised for local and national charities and the number of colleagues involved in various community initiatives. This data had to be submitted every quarter on the WIRE.

There were two main types of funding through the ASDA Foundation: Matching grants or applications for funding and Sustainable projects. Both categories required that the applicant shows significant fundraising efforts before applying for funding. They also require a number of ASDA Colleagues to have been involved in the fundraising process weather in store or outside, for example at a school or sports club.

The main difference between the two categories lay in the amounts you can apply for. For relatively small amounts, up to £2000, a matching funding application can be put in, to match what was raised for a good cause. These tended to be smaller fundraisers, typically raising between £500 to £1000. This type of application didn't required accountability or receipts from the charity to where the money will be used, instead it was considered a donation from the ASDA

48

Foundation. Strict guidelines were put in place on the type of charity and its reputation and all related documentation (e.g. Charity numbers, etc).

The second category, involved more cash and more work: Sustainable projects are projects that make a long lasting difference in the local community, and involve building or landscaping that will be there after the project is finished. This includes school playgrounds, historical buildings, community clubs, facilities, etc. The amounts can be up to £50,000 and a complete account of expenditure needs to be submitted to the Foundation. Volunteers need to do as much work as possible (e.g. painting, cleaning, etc), and the Foundation grant should be spent on materials rather than labour. One of the conditions of the funding as well is to involve various sections of the community in the project, and especially volunteers from ASDA. The foundation pays for the material through receiving the receipts and paying the suppliers directly if possible. We had significant success with this type of applications and they have much bigger impact in terms of local community benefit and marketing. These were projects that stayed on for years, and had plaques to commemorate ASDA's involvement. They were also much more appreciated locally, as people could see where the money was going on one hand, and due to the involvement of locals in the projects either directly through volunteers or indirectly, through people who benefited from the them, such as parents with their children in case of playgrounds or schools for example, or disabled facilities in a social club.

I guess it would be fair to say that Wal-Mart acquisition was one of the factors that created my job. In a way, the community involvement and social responsibility pushed by Wal-Mart really did set ASDA apart from all other supermarkets in the UK, and despite efforts from TESCO and Sainsbury's to follow, ASDA's early start and focus on the local community did pay off. So, after ten years, the Wal-Mart take-over did benefit ASDA, and despite the early teething problems, ASDA is now reaping the rewards. And considering that TESCO has almost eight times more stores, it only has less than double ASDA's market share (30% and 17% respectively, in 2009).

My role expanded into Sports for Children, schools programmes and healthy eating. It was all about the image of ASDA locally. And it did work. Later, many shoppers were telling me personally that ASDA's good work in the community makes them prefer to shop in it. It is all about customer perception. The public much prefer to be involved in local issues that affect them, rather than national issues hundreds of miles away and have no direct impact on the local community.

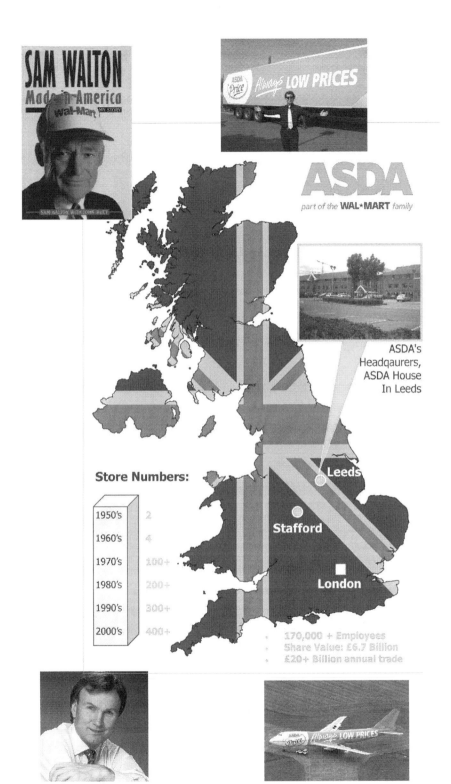

Store Numbers:

1950's	2
1960's	4
1970's	100+
1980's	200+
1990's	300+
2000's	400+

ASDA's
Headqaurers,
ASDA House
In Leeds

Leeds

Stafford

London

170,000 + Employees
Share Value: £6.7 Billion
£20+ Billion annual trade

The first WalMart Store in Bentonville, top and a typical WalMart store today.

Typical ASDA Store in the UK, check-outs, and the famous ASDA lorry!

Chapter Three

Magic and Glamour

In my job, I have always tried to turn simple events or fundraisers into big festivals or celebrations. I tried to invite local and national celebrities whenever possible and appropriate. This, in my opinion, has many benefits: first, the public take better to bigger events, as it gives more credibility to the cause, thus making fundraising more effective. It also encourages the public to engage with us and give more.

Secondly, it is essential for good press and media coverage, which could be even more important than the actual money raised. In many cases, we had small charities fundraising, but because of the size of the event and the interest from the media, those charities gain much more coverage than they would normally (if any). This leads to more exposure and more sponsors and possibilities for them. It opens doors and raises their profile. I had many thank you letters from organizations that we organized events for, thanking me personally for the excellent media and PR exposure they had through my work. We always turn event into mini festivals. That worked perfectly for both the charity and ASDA.

I remember in one of our regional meetings in 2009, I had 15 Events Coordinator from around the region to discuss our agenda for the next year; I prepared a presentation as the leader of the group about efficient event management. I presented my 3 G rule: Grab, Give and Get.

For a successful fundraiser or event, you need those 3G's. First, Grab people's attention, do something funny, dress up, use colourful props, a pink car, a huge toy animal. If people don't notice you in the first place, they won't listen or engage. Second, Give something back. People are fed up of giving and donating to so many charities. Everyone is asking for money. It would be much nicer to give them something first, to break the ice. Let it be a balloon for their kid, a free tooth brush or free sticker. This puts them in the mood for giving straight away. It also makes it easy for people to justify to themselves why they gave you and not somebody else and feel good about it too. You should also give enough clear information about where the money is going exactly. Finally, Get their money! If you follow the first two steps, then you should have no problem. Remember to smile all the time! It always helps the introductions.

Following the rules that I set for myself, I did exactly that. I turned many of the boring typical fundraisers into festivals, full of magic and glamour. I also tried as much as possible to use my connections and invite celebrities or local dignitaries, such as the Mayor or the local MP, local footballers, etc.

I tried to capture people's imagination and put them in a good mood when they come to ASDA. Up to this day, people come to me and remember me in this costume or that event.

Some people even bring me photos they took on one event or another and express how much they enjoyed it.

And that is exactly what I aimed to do: to make their shopping experience more enjoyable. That is the secret to the best marketing in the world. If they enjoy it, they will spend more and most importantly come back. Some customers told me they can't wait to see what we do next time they come shopping. To me, that is the greatest complement of all, and a proof that we succeeded in what we do and what we want to achieve.

In Sept. 2005, for my first event, I organized a fundraiser for Tickled Pink, the ASDA Breast cancer research campaign. I had everyone dressed in Pink, with various characters from the Fancy Dress shop (which I hired at extremely discounted prices, being for charity). I also raffled off a two-hour hire of a Pink Limousine! I got the prize for free in return of advertising the Wedding hire company. We had loads of pink balloons, banners, bunting everywhere, and the stretch Limo (the prize) was parked right at the front of the store for people to see their prize, they could also have pictures and sit in it for £1! We had free face painting and sweets for kids (Give). All in all, the event was a great success and we raised over £900 in one day, we had coverage in every newspaper in Stafford, and an interview live with me on Signal Radio (though I had to wake up at six o'clock in the morning for it, having slept only a few hours to prepare for the event and due to being anxious!).

That was truly a success with flying colours (mostly pink!).

Another significant event, which I remember fondly took place in 2008. It was the ASDA Stafford's store 10th Birthday, a big occasion for Stafford not only for ASDA. For that, I invited the Worshipful Mayor of Stafford Borough, and a very dear friend, Cllr Ann Edgeller and her Consort, Mr. Peter Edgeller to the event. She kindly agreed and launched the celebration. We had a specially made cake (I made myself out of 50 Swiss rolls, 10 Victoria sponge cakes and many marshmallows and much jam!). The cake was about 4 feet by 4 feet and was on the shape of Stafford Castle. I arranged for a Pink Cadillac (1959) with the big fins to be on display at the front of the store, and we had Rock'n'Roll music playing all day in the foyer. We had so many customers dancing in the foyer, and we raised money at the same time for Tickled Pink. Even the Mayor herself danced with me in the Foyer. This was filmed by the Express and Star newspaper crew and was on their website for many years. We had a special area cordoned off in the middle of the Foyer of the store; with music and many balloons for would be dancers! Customers could have cake pieces for free. We had a large banner at the front of the store, and specially made ASDA 10 Years balloons.

Another interesting but different event we had in 2008 was the launch of the new (then) James Bond film, Casino Royale. I dressed up in a Tuxedo as James Bond and we had a brand new BMW (on loan from the local BMW garage) and Porsches in the car park. We had some bubbly wine to give out and free posters with every DVD. We almost sold out of the new DVD on the first day.

Among the colourful events we had, were the national days of St. George's and St. Patrick's. It is a great and easy way to dress up and create a buzz. I dressed up as St. George's knight, and for St. Patrick's day, we had green and orange hats. Both events were covered in the local media more than once. They simply make a great picture! We even had shoppers involved, and some were happy to put a hat on for a funny picture!

In early 2010, we had the BBC Saturday Kitchen show filming in the wine aisle at ASDA Stafford. The renowned world class wine expert Tim Atkin was there, and I used the opportunity to introduce him to our customers, which created a buzz in the store. You don't meet a celebrity every time on your shopping trip!

One very different and interesting event we had in May 2010 was Belly Dancing! Yes, you read correctly. I was approached by a local dance teacher, who wanted to organize a fundraiser for the local Breast Care Unit at the Stafford hospital, a great local cause. The event was a Belly Dancing show at the local Church Hall, in Trinity Church in Stafford. First, I thought this could really backfire: Belly Dancing in ASDA Foyer to promote a show in a church hall! But she assured me it was all professional and not offending. So, I decided to take the risk and go for it! I thought it would definitely make a great story and a great photo for the papers, and that is always a good start! So I booked them in the foyer arranger for the photo call, and prepared the press release. I even called my contact in the local fancy dress shop and got a full Pharaoh's outfit to wear on the day (No, not a belly dancing suit!). The event went extremely well, and we had excellent coverage from the media. There were four lady belly dancers in the ASDA

Foyer, and me as the Pharaoh greeting shoppers. We had Arabic music playing in the Foyer, a picture gallery and several dance demos.

It was fantastic! Real glamour with their colourful professional costumes, and we had excellent feedback from the public. No complaints and we even had enquiries on Belly Dance classes! It certainly captured people's imagination and many stopped and watched the amazing dance routines. It was a gamble, but it paid off! In some cases, you have to follow your instinct. I must praise the support and trust of the general store manager, Mr. Chris Darby, in my judgement, for which I am very grateful.

Another different event I organized involved many colleagues in store in 2008: ASDA's Got Talent. We decided to run a talent competition in the Foyer of the Store for ASDA colleagues. We had a very good response with 14 acts entered. I did the dancing. We had Sister Act, Charlie Chaplin, Singers, A band, comedians, and many more. We borrowed a portable stage from the local Gatehouse Theatre and had some music and a sound system. Our restaurant manager, Terry presented the show (he was brilliant) and we ran the competition in front of the surprised customers in the Foyer at lunch time. For a whole hour, we entertained our shoppers and had many laughs. We raised some money, but most importantly, we had a good time and bonded with our shoppers. Even better, we had a front page photo and story in the Express and Star, Stafford's biggest selling newspaper.

Among the many promotions we had, I dressed up as Rocky Balboa, for the launch of the Stallone DVD, Harry Potter for two of the Harry Potter movies, Austin Powers, for Valentine's day, Ring master for Tickled Pink, Christmas Elf and Santa for Christmas, Pudsey the Bear for Children In Need, a Snow man, and even a Reindeer!

One important event in the Stafford calendar every year is the Mayor's Parade. Every July, businesses, charities and other organizations take part in a glamorous parade through the town centre; either on foot or on floats (decorated lorries) dressed up in colourful and funny costumes.   Every year there is a different theme: a children's play, theatre, local culture, animals,...etc.

Everyone makes an effort and the best display wins a prize.   The Mayor launches the parade and for two hours, everyone on the streets of Stafford stops and watches.   Streets are usually blocked for the duration of the parade.   On average, between 30 and 40 different displays and floats march through the town centre streets, and it turns it into a festival of colour and music.

We took part in the parade several times, always on a float.   One year, our theme was the little mermaid, and I spent hours in the ASDA Warehouse drawing and cutting out tens of huge Nemos and fishes and sea weeds to decorate the float! I used old card board from POS (Point of Sale) signs.

Another year, our theme was Ballet; I picked Swan Lake, and organized for 8 young dancers from a local Ballet school to come and dance on the float. We borrowed a generator and a sound system and I decorated the lorry with white and blue bed sheets to resemble the lake. All went well, until the sound system stopped working minutes before the start! I rushed to the local electrical shop and with no money on me, the guy knew me from the papers and lent me the required parts for free, I promised to pay him later and he trusted me. I did pay him back later.   Any way, it worked out, and we had excellent feedback and had a full page Photo in a picture special spread in the local newspaper of our dancers. If you are wondering what I dressed up as, I can tell you it was not a swan! I dressed up as the prince with my cape.   Everyone had great fun.

One year, as part of the Mayor's Parade, I used one of the contacts I had by the in the Council, who was the Marketing Coordinator for the Borough, and we set up a giant covered stage in the middle of the Market square. My vision was to run a competition to choose the Face of George, someone who would model for our clothing brand.   It was part of a national ASDA Competition, where applicants send their photo and a resume and the winner would be featured in an ASDA

George TV ad. But I took the initiative and took it a step further and got the local community involved. I saw an ample opportunity and potential for a great local PR story.

First, we announced the competition in the local media and got over 40 applicants. Then, we narrowed it to 8 people and organized a fashion cat walk on the stage in the town centre at the Mayors parade, complete with music and a professional presenter. I also had three judges to judge the finalists: the head of Marketing of the Local Saloon, Francesco Academy, George manager and a news fashion reporter.

The contestant had to do the catwalk in front of the crowd, each at a time, they were then interviewed and based on the judges' comments and crowd clapping, the winners were chosen. It was vibrant event and we really got the public engaged. We had large George Signs specially made and balloons giveaways and decorated the stage.

It was a great success, and the winner was a local primary school teacher. This event had a strong echo locally and people still remember it. It was also held on the busiest day of the year in Stafford at a prime time in the Mayor's parade.

My partner and I also did the entertainment during the break, which was a Latin Dance demo. It was a professional event that wouldn't look out of place in any big festival!

In 2009 we worked with the Forestry Commission to promote their summer concerts in Cannock chase, that year it was the Sugababes. We held a competition to win tickets to the concert and had their leaflets promoted in the store.

At the launch of Hannah Montana movie in 2008 we ran a competition for children to win a holiday in L.A., USA, and stage tickets to a Hannah Montana show. I also asked one of our Staff, whose daughter (like many girls) was really a fan of the character. She dressed up like Hannah on the day, and helped me promote the competition in the Foyer. We had a good photo in the paper, and gave out tens of competition entries.

Christmas time is always a magical and special time and many shops and companies get into the spirit of Christmas. We too at ASDA always have the decorations, the Tree, and the banners, even a special red uniform for Christmas. I was also in charge of organizing the Colleagues Christmas Party, which sometimes took place in January. Because I knew many businesses in town, I always got the best rates for hiring the venue. But I also wanted to do something extra, and more in the heart of the community. I wanted to go the extra mile.

In Dec. 2009, with the Stafford Organ Society, we organized a promotion day for the society in the Foyer of ASDA. I worked with the President, Derek Sharp and we invited Jean Martyn, the world famous organist and pianist, and is number one in the UK. She kindly agreed and came for a Saturday performance for whole 3 hours into ASDA Foyer, where we setup an organ for her under our huge 15 feet Christmas tree. Just two days prior to coming to play in ASDA, she was performing for HRH the Prince of Wales, at St. James' Palace in London. She is also the only woman to perform on the organ of the legendary Blackpool Tower. We had excellent response from the public and the event was covered in the local media.

We also had Choirs from local Schools singing in the Foyer on several occasions, particularly during the Stafford Music Festival.

That same year, 2009, we helped organize a Christmas Tree Festival inside the St. Mary's Church in Stafford town Centre.

St. Mary's Church is Stafford's Biggest Church, and the Oldest in the UK. One of the organs is world renowned with thousands of original pipes, and there is ongoing effort to restore it. It is situated right in the centre of the town, with easy access to the shopping areas and the main street. So, it was an ideal venue for such an event, where people can simply come and have a look while they are shopping or during their lunch break.

I knew the Vicar at the Church personally as well as Stafford's Town Centre Chaplin and we organized for 50 Christmas trees to be set up inside the church. Local businesses can then buy a tree and decorate to advertise the business. All proceeds went to charity. There was also a competition for the best tree, to be voted by the public. There were refreshments, coffee and tea (donated by ASDA) and collection tins.

It was a different but super event, right in the heart of the town, and we had excellent public and media response. I even dressed up as an elf and we had one of the best trees there (even if I say so!). We raised over £1500 and the Mayor of Stafford opened the event. It not only brought the community together, but also all local businesses side by side in a festival of light and magic. Even the Police and many voluntary services took part in the event. The event also helped to raise St. Mary's Church profile as a community centre.

While on the subject of Christmas, we used to do a Santa's Hospital round every year, in collaboration with the Hospital League of Friends charity. I used to dress up as a Santa or an Elf, and along with two or three other colleagues, we used go around the Children's Ward in Stafford Hospital giving children who are at the hospital during Christmas presents. The presents were jointly donated by the League of Friends and ASDA.

It was a really magical time, and children were genuinely surprised, as we didn't even tell parents beforehand. We had the local MP with us many times and the Mayor of Stafford.

Another part of the Christmas magic every year is the Panto at the local Theatre. It is a big event and the play runs for several weeks and every child in Stafford waits for it. In Nov. 2009, we sponsored and supported the Cinderella play at the Gatehouse Theatre. We provided the sweets, goody bags and other items to be given out to the children at the end of each performance. We then invited all the characters from the play to the ASDA Foyer to promote the play, and the same time raise money for Breast Cancer Research. It was a win-win situation and children loved seeing their favourite characters dressed up live in the local Supermarket!   Many were stopping and taking pictures.   As one of the main sponsors we had a large ad in the Panto guide which was seen by almost every family in Stafford during the show.   Our logo was also featured on all the posters, banners and leaflets for the play.   I also got over 100 free tickets for our staff to see the show, for which they were grateful!   And the PR value was massive.

In another Tickled Pink fundraiser in Sept. 2007; I organized a themed day at the store.   The theme was Grease! One of my all time favourite movies, and appropriately, there is lots of scope for pink: the Pink Ladies, Pink Cadillacs, pink shirts and Rock'n'Roll.   We had a volunteer DJ in the foyer, Johnny, who is great on Rock'n'Roll and actually runs the Stafford Rock'n'Roll club.

On the day, the Mayor of Stafford launched the event by cutting the big Tickled Pink cake, in the Foyer of ASDA.   We had Rock'n'Roll music and colleagues dressed up in characters from the movie.   The local MP, Mr. David Kidney kindly joined us.   It was a fantastic and magical event. We had a Pink Cadillac at the front of the store too.

The Mayoress of Stafford at that time, Mrs. Price got really involved in the event and was a great supporter of the charity. She had beaten Breast Cancer herself and it was a cause that is close to her heart. She even helped us with the collection at the front of the store.   The shoppers really appreciated that and donated generously.

I have always strived to generate a bigger impact through more magical and glamorous events, as that in my opinion is the only way to maximise both funds raised and the media coverage. It worked every time.

Some of characters I've been or met in various events.

Below: during a BBC filming in-store.

St. George's Day, Face of George Event, with the Stig, James Bond Casino Royale launch and the Chinese new year.

Various Tickled Pink fundraisers over the years, with different Mayors and Stafford MP David Kidney (middle).

Above: The Orien-
tal Theme Belly
Dancing fundraiser
in the Foyer of
ASDA Stafford,
which we used later
in the Mayor's pa-
rade in 2010.

Left: The Cinderella
Panto promotion
with teh local Gate-
house Theatre in the
ASDA Stafford
store in 2009.

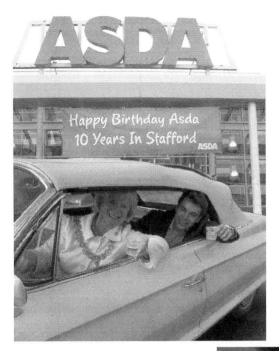

Top left: Celebrating 10 years of ASDA in Stafford.
Below: Best float award in the Mayor's Parade in 2010.

Below: World famous organist, Jean Martyn playing in ASDA Staford Foyer, Christmas 2009. Top right, and bottom right: Christmas gifts appeal, at the children's ward in the Hospital.

Above: The Mayor's Parade float in 2007, themed Swan Lake, we had dancers from the local dance school. Below: The Sheriff of ASDA and the Christmas gift appeal.

Chapter Four

Fastest, Strongest, ... Best!

In Public Relations (PR), a good story is half the battle. If someone can lift a car single handed that is a story. If someone lifts a car in front of your local super market, full of shopping, that is a great story! Not only you get big exposure due to the number of people passing through the doors, but it is great indirect publicity.

People love extremes. Anything different attracts people's attention. People also love the underdog story and achievements. If you link that to a good cause, then you absolutely have a PR dream.

Every now and then someone attempts a record or a challenge for charity or a good local cause that is bit different. That is exactly the kind of event that could make an effective story that people would talk about for weeks and months. It echoes and people remember it.

In summer 2006, I was approached by two guys to sponsor a kids fun day at Rowley park in Stafford. It is a big open area, with play areas, a stadium and tennis courts, that is open to the public. From the conversation on the phone, they asked for fruits and water to give out on the day for the children and the athletes who perform on the day. Part of the activities, was a Strong Man competition. My immediate reaction was that this is a good story!

When I met the two chaps, and had a chat with them about what they do, I was pleasantly surprised: One of them was actually Britain's strongest man a year before, and the other guy was his manager. They are giving something back to the community by organizing the fun day and mini competition in Stafford.

To me, that was the perfect PR opportunity and I grabbed it! I agreed to sponsor the event; in return we would have our healthy eating signs at the arena. But most importantly, I arranged for him to come into the store to promote the event beforehand. To me that was the story and the main PR potential.

So a couple of weeks before the event, we arranged for a brand new Kia Picanto car from the local garage to be set up on the ASDA Car Park, in front of the main store entrance. We filled the boot of the car with ASDA shopping bags, and Britain's Strongest Man lifted the car in front of the amazed shoppers! He even lifted me above his head! I coordinated the colour of the car, to be red, so it gives a good contrast with the green ASDA sign and his blue outfit.

It was a great stunt, and we had some great photos and great media response. It had all the right ingredients for a great store. It also helped boost the attendance at the events itself two weeks later, which I attended.

It was a different event; people don't see that every day. It had the wow factor. There was a celebrity involved (Britain's Strongest man), and it was appealing to the younger generation. It also promoted sports and exercise, which is one of our main goals. It promoted healthy eating and fruits. Above all that, it made a great photo! It was an example of a win-win situation.

Another interesting event started as a charity fundraiser and ended up with a world Guinness Record. Ray Edensor, a local paramedic from Stafford wanted to raise money for the Midlands Air Ambulance. Coincidently, that year (2009) it was our supported charity too. His idea was to run 25 half-marathons in 25 days around Stafford. The twist was he'd do it in an anti-contamination suit!

When Ray contacted in late 2008, I thought there was great potential in this. It is a very good cause and people would be very willing to give. At the same time, the event itself is very different, and if we had the Guinness World record attempt as well, it will make it a super story. I met Ray several time the following weeks and months since our initial meeting, and we prepared a plan for the campaign. I call it that because it wasn't a one day event, so we had to orchestrate the events to get the most PR coverage we could.

So, decided to the hold a press conference at ASDA in February 2009, to tell the media and the papers about what we intend to do. At the same time, Ray would be weighed officially, to check his weight before and after the run.

The weighting and the press conference went very well, and we even had a filming crew to film the process. We had a massive front page article with a photo of Ray in front of ASDA on the scales.

The second stage was the marathons themselves. We coordinated it to be in conjunction with the Stafford annual Half marathon, which was also celebrating 25 years that year. We requested from the organizers for Ray to have number 25 on his suit, and they did. At the same time, we had the ASDA logo on his suit as the main sponsor.

Throughout the 25 days of the running, everyone in Stafford saw Ray in his anti-contamination suit running up and down the streets of Stafford. Everyone in Stafford was talking about it and the amount of publicity was immense.

Ray managed to finish the marathons, and set a new Guinness world record. The media response was fantastic. He raised £4500 for the Air Ambulance and we donated £1500 to top up his total to £6000. We had a cheque presentation ceremony at ASDA in the Foyer, with three big cheques and representatives of the charity. It was a very good photo.

That was not the first time I met Ray though. He is well known in Stafford for his relentless pursuit of challenges to raise money for charity. He is dubbed the Running Paramedic and was featured on the

BBC for his various challenges. He raised tens of thousands of pounds for various good local causes.

I met Ray back in 2007, when he approached me for a fundraiser he was doing for the Stafford Hospital. He came across as a nice quietly spoken person, but he had big ideas and I like that.

His challenge was to raffle off a brand new car, and do an Ambulance bed push through town to promote it and raise money for it. I felt it was a good story and raffling a car is always catchy! So we used our contacts and arranged a car to be donated through the local Peugeot garage (Mike Thompson), who kindly donated a bright yellow Peugeot 1007, city car. The colour was important as we decided to display the car at the front of the store for a week to advertise the raffle.

We launched the raffle at the Peugeot garage, with excellent press coverage. The car was then on display at ASDA, where people could by the tickets too.

On the day of the Mayor's parade in 2008, Ray and two other paramedics pushed an ambulance bed from ASDA to the Market Square in Stafford, passing through the town centre. The Mayor of Stafford launched the bed push by cutting the ribbon at the front of the ASDA foyer, along with the commander of the Air Ambulance in Staffordshire and other guests. It was a fantastic send off. The new car followed Ray and his paramedic team mates around Stafford.

This event raised over £8,000 for charity and I arranged for the winner of the car to receive his prize at ASDA in Sept. 2008.

While we are on the subject of World records, another fascinating event we supported had a similar theme. A lady approached me in store in late 2009, saying that she saw me in the papers supporting various charities and wondered if I could be of help to her. I asked her to come and meet me.

To my surprise, she said that she is asking for help on behalf of her daughters, Jo and Dannii, who have the idea of organizing a fundraiser for the British Heart Foundation in May 2010, by breaking the World Guinness Record for the longest continuous darts games! I was amazed by the big task they set for themselves, but I felt it was a very good cause and if it happens, it will be a great PR opportunity.

So, in early 2010, I met Jo and Dannii Tonks, two sisters from Stafford, who are also very good Darts players! They started to explain to me the motivation behind the challenge: a very dear friend and neighbour died recently, but he had massive support from the British Heart Foundation, and they felt they wanted to do something to thank BHF for what they did.

So they decided to break the World Record! To be fair, I wasn't sure in the beginning that they can pull off all the logistics, the judges and witnesses needed for a 30 hours continuous Darts marathon. But they were very determined and organized, so I felt I have to help them. They were also a very close family, and their dad, mum and aunt were all helping them. So I felt that with a team like that, they can make it.

On the other hand, it was a great story: Two sisters from Stafford breaking a World Guinness Record to raise money for the BHF.

I was impressed when they told me that they already have a couple of sponsors, Red Bull, and a Darts manufacturer. To me, that was a good sign, and we agreed that we at ASDA will support them and sponsor them. I also helped them with the PR side, and used my local contacts in the media to arrange the photo calls and press releases.

I arranged for them to come to ASDA in the Foyer to tell the public about what they do and raise more money through sponsorship. We set up a very colourful display and they had the four of them (mum, aunt and the two sisters) had the BHF red t-shirts. They also displayed information about darts, a couple of dart boards and some leaflets. It was a good event and helped boost their confidence and spread the word.

On the day of the attempt, 30th April 2010, I remember it well as it was my birthday; they started at 10:00am, at the Social Club in St. George Hospital in Stafford. They had a stage prepared with a dart board and lights, music and lots of red balloons. The public could come in at any time and watch them and hopefully make donations. I brought them some food and snacks, drinks and bits for their buffet the next day.

They played non-stop through the night and the next day, 1st May 2010; at 6:21pm they finished and beat the World Guinness Record by 3 full hours! Everyone in the club and around the bar cheered, including me, there tears of joy, lots of pain but everyone was extremely happy. After the photos and the cakes, wine and tears, the girls finally sat down and reflected on what they did. I told them they made history in Stafford, and they really have.

The event was covered in all local papers, local radio and front pages. A few weeks later, they organized a thank you party at the same place, and announced the total: £3160, they beat their target of £3000, and set a new World Guinness record.

It was a real inspiration working with the two sisters and I personally enjoyed the whole experience. It was a privilege to be part of this massive achievement.

Another major challenge I witnessed and was part of, was a big corporate fundraiser for Pedal Power. It is a national charity, set up by ASDA with Sport Aid UK, to encourage young people to use their bicycles and exercise more outdoors. It supports local cycling clubs across the UK. It was pushed by Andy Bond, the CEO of ASDA between 2005 and 2010, being a keen cyclist himself. The patron of the Charity is Sir Chris Hoy, the Olympic gold medallist cyclist.

The company set a corporate challenge to raise £1 million in 2009, and everyone started to come up with ideas. We held a lot of fundraisers locally. But the main event was Any Bond, cycling from Land's End to John O'Grote (over 1000 miles) from the farthest northern point in the UK to the most southern. He would be joined by a group of professional cyclists and Sir Chris Hoy. On the way, they stop at every ASDA on the route.

I helped organise the reception at ASDA Shrewsbury for the cyclists as they come in on the way. The Mayor of Shrewsbury was present and representatives from 15 stores around the region. A big cheer was planned on their arrival and lots of drinks! There was also a buffet set up.

When they arrived, we presented Andy Bond with a cheque of the total raised by the region, and it was in excess of £80,000.

The total raised for Pedal Power in 2009 was over £1.3 million, well above the target and the campaign went well. In my opinion though, such a high profile campaign did not get the national coverage it deserved. The bike ride alone should have been covered nationally, with celebrities like Sir Chris Hoy on board; it could have been a great PR exercise. Instead, ASDA PR team relied on local coverage, which in this case was not sufficient, and the cause itself was not local, so many people didn't understand or couldn't relate to the events.

Funny enough, exactly the same bike ride took place just a month later for the BBC Children in need by presenters and it had massive coverage.

It also didn't help that the charity was just born, and no one knew about it before. A national campaign would have been the perfect start in my opinion. It first push is always the hardest, and once people know about it, then it will snow ball.

Don't get me wrong, I think the idea behind the charity is great, and the bike ride was a great way to raise money. It is the handling of the PR was too decentralized that it lost its momentum. In some cases, we didn't even have banners or posters to display for customers in the store about the campaign. It caused some confusion for the shoppers. I had to design my own posters and leaflets and print them locally.

Top: promoting Guinness World record marathon run in an anti-contamination suit, with Ray Edensor.

Left: World strongest man event.

Below: Pedal power with Andy Bond, and Guinness record in Darts.

Chapter Five

On Your Marks, set, ... Go!

An important part of my job was not just support charities and good causes, but also to promote sports and healthy life style for children.

The main focus was to reach out to the local community and encourage and support local initiatives in sports and physical activities.

One very successful and massive event we have every year, is the national Kwick Cricket competition. ASDA teams up with the England Cricket Board and together they organize the biggest under 16s Cricket tournament in the UK. Over 150,000 children take part across the UK. ASDA sponsors the event and provides the fruit and water for the players. ASDA also provides the schools with the cricket kits and t-shirts and caps for children to wear at the games. One of our sponsors last year was Buxton Water who supplied the water.

The event usually runs between May and July each year. Schools compete locally, and the finalists from each county then play against each other in the county finals. The winning teams from across the UK then compete for the Trophy in a national final.

We have organized the Staffordshire County Finals for three consecutive years and had great success and excellent feedback. Each time, we have about 120 to 150 children, with their parents. We usually have a professional celebrity Cricketer on the day to talk to the children and sign their kit. At the end of the day, they hold a Q&A session about cricket.

The event usually starts at 10:00am and Finished at 4:00pm. Our finals are held at the Modder shall Cricket Ground near Stone, which is a few miles outside Stafford.

I liaise with the local Cricket Officer to confirm the numbers and locations, and I usually handle the PR and the press releases.

In all the competitions I co-organized, the children seem to have great fun and it is really a nice day for the whole family. I was personally told by many parents how grateful they are to ASDA for organizing and sponsoring these events. Some schools cannot afford the kit and in many cases, the organizational aspect of these events is too much for one school.

Another memorable and very local initiative I was involved in organizing was the Staffordshire County Under 9s Rugby Finals in April 2010. The Stafford Rugby club relies mainly on volunteers and parents to run. These are a nice group of people who want the best for their children and really get behind them. They have over 300 under 9s members.

I was approached by one of the parent organizers, Helen Pearson, a lovely lady, to help sponsor their lunch boxes. After meeting with her, she explained that they are actually hosting the County finals and they have ten Rugby teams playing in Stafford. They had no experience in organizing such a big event and were struggling.

I felt enthusiastic about the event and I could see there is PR potential for ASDA, but at the same time I genuinely wanted to help them. They have come so far by landing the organization of the County finals, which is quite a big event. I also felt their work should be celebrated and made known to the people of Stafford. I felt they needed help with PR.

So, we had a couple of meetings, I arranged for 150 lunch boxes for them, including water and fruits, and the cardboard children's boxes which I got from our restaurant. I also arranged the press releases and invited the local media to the event. I invited the Mayor of Stafford, Cllr Jean Taberner, who kindly launched the event.

We had a display at the ASDA Foyer a couple of weeks prior, to raise awareness. Ten children and parents all in their lovely Black and Yellow uniforms spent four hours in the foyer of ASDA.

On the day, 18th April 2010, we had excellent weather. The Mayor launched the event at the Stafford Rugby Club and all the teams were there on time. We had very good press coverage, and I turned it into a local story not just for the Rugby Club, but an event for all of Stafford to be proud of. And it was. Everyone was so grateful for my help, I actually felt embarrassed.

A week later, the club invited me to present the awards for the end of the season, and to my surprise, they presented me with my own Rugby shirt! That was such a lovely gesture, and I had a lovely time. I will always remember this lovely group of people.

The club was grateful for ASDA's support, and we got excellent coverage and a full page advertisement in the game guide. This was seen by over 500 people. A great result for everyone.

We have been involved in cricket and rugby but what about football you may ask? Well, we were heavily involved with our local football club, the Stafford Rangers FC. I realized from the start the potential of football. Football club are a brilliant platform for marketing, due to the large number of fans and local impact. The stadium is a good start: throughout the season thousands of local supporters pass through the gates, and any advertising will have a massive impact.

So, since 2006, we supplied over 10,000 water bottles to the Stafford Ranges FC, three full season's water supply for the players. In return, we had a permanent ASDA board behind one of the goals at the Stafford Rangers grounds. We had very good PR coverage as well, with interesting stories.

When Steve Bull MBE, the Wolves football legend joined the Rangers as the manager in 2007, they choose ASDA Stafford to launch their new kit. That was an exciting event, with many fans turning up at the store for signing and we had a big Stan Robinson Lorry on display at the ASDA car park (it is a haulage company and he is one of the main sponsors of the Rangers). The chairman of the club, Jon Downing and various sponsors were also present. It was a high profile event, and the media response was excellent as you would expect.

Later in the year, we worked with the Stafford Rangers FC on their Junior training sessions, and we donated 100 footballs for their Junior club.

The relationship with the Stafford Rangers was ongoing, and I tried to boost it because I felt the club was a landmark of Stafford, with over 100 years of history and thousands of supports.

In 2009, I worked with the Club chairman, Mr. Jon Downing on an exciting and ambitious project. The vision was to transform the social club building at the Stafford Rangers FC into a venue that would be in the heart of the community as a meeting point for local people and groups, as well as functions and other youth activities. The building itself has suffered from neglect over the year and had no disabled facilities, which further limited its prospects.

In Sept. 2009, we organized a high profile bike ride, to raise money for the project. We estimated the budget between £10,000 to £15,000. Most of the work was to be carried out by volunteers and money to be spent on material when possible.

The bike ride gained momentum and we soon had 100+ people. Jon Downing used his contacts and we had Eleanor Simmonds OBE, the Olympic Paralympics swimmer (who won Gold in 2008) on the day. She launched the event. The Mayor of Stafford gave the prizes and we had many photographers and local press representatives present on the day.

The starting line was in the Market Square, and the finish line was at the Stafford Rangers FC. It was a 10 Km ride. I took part myself so did Jon Downing. We raised a total of £6000 and we raised the profile of the project, so much, that we had companies coming forward donating materials.

We then applied for funding to the ASDA Foundation, as I believed it was an exemplar sustainable project to benefit the local community. We managed to secure £5000 and the project took off. I arranged for a photo call and a press release about it, and I spent four hours building a 3ft X 3ft card board model of the Social Club Building in its finished form. We had coverage in all local papers.

The money was to be spent on refurbishing the social club, installing disabled facilities and general cleaning and decorating.

My instinct was right and I had so much favourable feedback from people in Stafford praising ASDA's support for the project, and emphasizing the difference it would make locally. I knew that football is close to many people's hearts and the project will have good impact in terms of PR.

While on the subject of the Football club, on Sun. 25th April 2010, we helped organize a big charity football game at the club between the Wolves All Stars and Stoke City Old Boys. The charity was NACCPO (National Alliance for Childhood Cancer Parents Organizations), which is based in Stafford. The old players from both team put their shirts on for one last performance to raise money for the charity.

The Mayor of Stafford launched the events, and over 1000 people attended on the day, including many families and children. There was also a display of star wars troopers (fans from the Star Wars fan club who volunteered to dress up and bring their gear for the day). There was also an evening event at the Social Club (including Buffet and entertainment for guests and players).

The event raised over £4000, and in my opinion was very successful.

Another very different sporting event I was involved in, is the Right Stuff project. A local Policeman started a youth club to get youth off the street and get them involved in something useful. So the idea was to launch a boxing club, to get rid of the aggression off the street. The project grew over a few months, and the club acquired a derelict building north of Stafford. Volunteers renovated the building and through donations and fundraising, the club was equipped with professional boxing equipment. The Police also supported the project.

The new premises were officially opened in July 2009, in the presence of many high profile guests, including the prospective parliamentary Candidate for Stafford, Jeremy Lefroy, Cllr Ray Barron the County Councillor for the area and the Staffordshire Police Commissioner.

On a different note, and part of ASDA's policy of promoting sports for kids, every year in April we launch our Sporting Chance initiative. Parents at the checkouts of ASDA can pick up vouchers for free sporting sessions in hundreds of venues across the UK. These include leisure centres, sports clubs, sailing, tennis, swimming and many more.

These sessions were provided through partnership with local sports and leisure centres. My job was to find suitable venues locally and negotiate a deal. We then launched local campaigns to promote the scheme. A dedicated website was setup so that parents can find their local sessions providers easily and use their vouchers. This was updated with new venues as and when.

In Stafford, we had the Stafford Leisure Centre right behind the store, so that was one of the first ideal venues. The leisure centre gets the publicity and exposure on our national website in return for the sessions. We managed the scheme on their behalf as a well as handling all local PR. As part of the deal, they could also come onto ASDA and promote their business. This worked across the UK.

Overall, hundreds of thousands of free sessions were awarded across the country. The scheme generated good PR for ASDA, but did suffer from rival schemes from TESCO. It also didn't help that many local councils had their own free sporting sessions on offer.

Another aspect of the Sporting Chance scheme was an initiative that ASDA started with Sports Aid, to sponsor and support young promising and local athletes.

Sports Aid is a national sporting charity that sponsored promising athletes like Dame Kelly Holmes in their early careers. Through the scheme, young people can apply for a grant based on their sporting achievements. Two athletes are then chosen per year per store, and each receives £500 to help towards their equipment.

We had several successful launches, including Lauren Bromley, a local Badminton champion and Jasmine Royle, a Canoeing champion. One of the press photos showed Jasmine rowing in an ASDA trolley in front of my Stafford store.

An Ad I designed for a sporting event we sponsored.

Top left: Staffordshire County under 9's Rugby Finals, with Mayor Cllr Jean Taberner.

Top right: Sporting chance promo with the Gym.

Right: Charity Cycling, with Eleanor Simmonds OBE, Stafford MP Jeremy Lefroy .

Bottom: donating 100 footballs to Rangers, with Steve Bull MBE.

Below: The new social club model, with Jon Downing, Stafford Rangers FC Chairman.

Top left: Sporting chance
grant presentation to a
young athlete.
Above: Stafford Rangers
FC new kit launch in
2010.

Above: New Stafford Rangers FC kit launch
in 2008, at ASDA with Wolves legend and
Rangers manager Steve Bull MBE.
Right: Free health checks in the Foyer.

Top : Celebrating the Olympic year, with Alison Williamson , MBE, and the Mayor of Stafford, Cllr Bryan Cross MBE in June 2012 , just before the Olympics. In July 2012, Alison took part in her sixth Olympic games in London 2012, representing Team GB in Archery. She was made an MBE a week after that photo was took! Alison was one of the Olympic torch bearers and she brought it to ASDA Stafford. We organized a farewell event for her.

Bottom right: In the foyer of the Stafford store, promoting sports with Alison Williamson in 2011, before London 2012.

2012: Olympic year!

Top : With the actual Olympic Torch in the Foyer of the Stafford ASDA. I was determined to get the Torch into the store, and we were one of only a handful of stores to have the torch on show for the public. We were featured in ASDA's internal magazine too, and had a thank you letter from the ASDA Boss.

We had shoppers queuing for a photo with the torch and at some point blocked the entrance, and the security officers had to come and clear the way!

Bottom: With Olympic Torch Bearer , Caitlin Moon, who was one of the Torch bearers in Staffordshire.

Chapter Six

Young, Old .... and Different

Sports and charities were not the only aspects of community that we covered. In fact, the community programme I was responsible for covered all aspects of life in Stafford. I wanted to broaden the spectrum and worked hard to find potential new partnerships. I visited schools, hospitals, attended council meetings, charity AGM's and even political rallies. Everything was on the table, and the more unusual it is the better.

This meant that I was involved with over 20 different charities, six sports clubs, seven schools, the local council, the local theatre, the hospital and many other local organizations.

I was never short of a story, and in fact, in some cases, I had press releases and stories for several months ahead. I always had three or more projects on the go. My diary used to be filled up for months ahead.

Every Mother's Day, we donated 100 goody bags to the Hospital for new mums, we also donated goody bags to the local Nursery. These bags included wet wipes, nappies, tooth brushes and other useful items.

Throughout the year, we had several healthy eating initiatives, including the lunch bunch promotion. I also visited schools locally to promote healthy eating and hold tasting sessions for fruit at school. We had several school visits to the store every year to show the children the different types of fruit and fresh vegetables, as well information on how to understand the labels on the fruit and the types and shapes of each sort.

In some cases we had up to 30 kids walking around the store in a train with their teachers and I presented to them the different sections. We also had other colleague from relevant departments present their products.

I also arranged for school visits with local Dental practices, to talk to children about the importance to taking care of their teeth. That was usually during the NHS Smile month every year in May.

We also ran NHS Stop Smoking campaigns at the store, giving out free stop smoking information, advice and goods. We often had free health checks at the front of the store, which I used arrange with local health clubs, such as Esporta.

In Easter, we always had a celebration in store with free chocolate eggs giveaways, face painting and the famous Easter Bonnet parade.

In 2008, a lady in Stafford celebrated her 100th Birthday, and we provided the special cake for her. I found out she liked chocolate, so we donated a lovely chocolate fudge cake that she loved!

In 2010, the Oddfellows Charity, with its Mid Staffs branch the Oddfellows Hall in Greengate Street, Stafford, has celebrated 200 years today, 1810-2010, a great milestone. The charity hosts a variety of events for the community and looks after its members through a series of events and services. They also raise funds for various good causes with branches all over the world.

I knew the secretary, Karen Simms, she contacted me and we donated the special celebration cakes with the Oddfellow crests to cater for over 200 people.

One of our colleagues who worked on counters, Linda, turned 60, so we arranged a surprise party for her and I dressed up as a Cowboy Sherriff and arrested her! The papers loved the story, and we had a photo in the paper with a caption saying: The Sherriff of ASDA arrests Linda!

Every year we support the Poppy Appeal, through donations and collections, and we usually have a stand in the foyer with ex-servicemen. We did the same with the Servicemen, Seamen and Air Force Association (SSAFA).

I am proud to say that in Stafford, we have been very successful in attracting funding from the ASDA Foundation, and we have completed a string of successful community projects that made a real difference to the local community and excellent publicity for ASDA. I had a special relationship with the Foundation manager, Julie Ward, who trusted my judgement and endorsed our funding applications. This was then strengthened through the excellent PR coverage I made sure we get for every project to maximise the impact. She told me personally that the amount of press cuttings we got here was more than other projects around the country that had five or six times the amount of funding we had in some cases.

Projects that benefited young people and children were a top priority for the foundation and rightfully so. Children are the future and focusing on them is an investment in the future.

In 2006, we obtained funding through a grant from the ASDA Foundation to refurbish and update a sensory garden at the local Marshlands Special School. It was my first project to be funded through the ASDA Foundation. I arranged for volunteers to work on the garden, and we got the materials and equipment. The garden was abandoned for many years and it would make a big difference to the children at that school.

We spent weeks cleaning and building, and restoring the garden and the different sculptures and paths. I designed the new layout and landscaping, then I choose a bright colour scheme to make it more fun for the children. I even used one of the areas to create an open air disco. We also had a windmill, stone animals and a fish pond.

The project was very successful and we had the local MP and the Mayor at the opening. We had coverage by every local newspaper throughout the different stages of the project.

At the end, the school invited me to join the board of Governors, and since then I've been a governor at the school.

The relationship with the school did not end there, I tried to help them in every possible occasion, and we sponsored their summer fetes, celebration lunches and many other events. In 2008 we obtained another grant from the ASDA Foundation, and we launched the Christmas card project.

We launched a competition among the pupils to design their own Christmas cards, and the top three designs were then professionally printed. I modified them a bit and had 5000 cards printed. These were then sold to raise funds for the school. The children were so excited to see their own design printed! Again, we had very good press coverage. The success of the project prompted us to repeat it in 2010, with another grant from the ASDA Foundation.

I was quite involved with the school, and being a governor and attending the governors meeting, I saw the great service this school provides to those special children. But it was also frustrating to see the funding cuts the school faced (as did many others) in their budgets. In 2008 the school lost two teaching posts. This reached its climax in early 2010 when the school was about to lose another Teaching Assistant.

I organized the parents and governors and decided to strike back using the tool that I know well: PR. We organized a petition to be signed by all the parents and to be sent to the Schools Secretary, Mr. Ed Balls at that time. We also launched a campaign in the local papers, and I arranged for a photo call of some of the parents holding a large S.O.S. sign made by the children. I called the campaign: Save Our School!

The campaign was covered by all local papers, and it was so powerful that the local MP at that time, Mr. David Kidney visited the school and held a meeting with me and the Head teacher, Ms Belinda Whale to discuss the situation. We also had (for once) replies from the Education authorities and the County Council.

I was so proud that I could help and make a difference. If anything, this campaign put the school on the map and may prevent future drastic cuts. It also brought the issue to the open, and clarified the situation to many of the parents.

On a lighter note, another successful project we completed with the ASDA Foundation in 2008 was the Walton Village Play ground. Walton is a village on the outskirts of Stafford and it had the only playground for children within a three mile radius. It was in a bad state of repair and needed new equipment, safety surfaces and general refurbishment.

I was originally approached by a resident mom, Emma Jane Wheatly, who was very enthusiastic about the project, for food donations for a walk to raise money for the project. When I met her, and realized that the total cost would be over £20,000, I knew straight away that they need more than a few fundraisers and they would take years to raise the money.

I found out that the County and Parish councils managed to allocate £10,000 for the project and they need another £10,000 to go ahead. I saw the potential of the project and its benefit to the community as well as the possible PR impact.

I wasted no time and put together a comprehensive application for funding to the ASDA Foundation for £10,000. I was delighted a couple of months later to get a phone call from Julie Ward, the Foundation manager to tell me that the trustees approved the funding and we beat over 70 other projects to it! Julie later came and visited the site.

The project was very successful, and the new play area opened in on the 13th September 2008, in a record three months, with the Deputy Mayor Cllr. Brian Cross (who later became my fellow Rotarian in the Stafford Knot Rotary Club), the Parish Council Chairman and the parent and their children.   We organized a picnic for everyone and celebrated the achievement.   There is still plaque there to this day acknowledging ASDA's contribution. We had front page coverage on the local papers.

Another interesting but different project involving young people in 2008/2009 was the games room at the Silkmore Partnership for Youth (SPY).   I was approached by a volunteer and a Police officer for donations for a summer fete they were organizing to raise money for a youth programme they started a few years back.

SPY relies on volunteers to create a safe environment for young people in the Silkmore area of Stafford, to meet weekly (on a Tuesday) and play games, sports, have a snack and generally to keep them off the streets and grow the community spirit.

I helped them with the buffet, and attended the day, were the Deputy Mayor Cllr Malcolm Millichap was present.   The held it at the local school, Silkmore Community Primary school.   We had a bouncy castle, a climbing wall, raffles, games a buffet, a fire engine and much more.   I also performed a Latin dance demonstration with my partner Karen, as we do Latin and ballroom dance as a hobby.   It was a lovely day and we raised a considerable amount which went back to SPY, and we also had very good press coverage.   This has then enabled me to put in a successful application for funding, fund a full state-of-the-art gaming room, for a Wii Sports system, complete with big 80" screen and projector, all the Wii attachments including boards and bats, games etc.   We also got the Wii sports and Wii fit.   We had a surround sound system too.

The room was housed in the Silkmore School, and the idea was to keep young people off the streets, doing something they like, and at the same time exercising an practicing sports in a different way. It is also useful when it is raining (which is quite often!).

When the room was officially opened, I helped install the system myself (my background is computing, and I used assemble PC's in my university placement). We had over 20 children queuing to try the new games room! They spent hours and enjoyed every minute. I did too!

One project I enjoyed working on was the Young Enterprise Programme between 2009 and 2010. It is a scheme run by the government to encourage entrepreneurship in High schools among pupils.

Interested pupils are divided into teams, each of which has to come up with an idea for a product. They then have to manage the project from start to end, including all the phases of Product development, design, marketing, manufacturing and eventually sales. It lasts for four to five months and at the end, they need to sell the products for a profit. The teams are then judged locally and nationally and winners are given attractive awards.

Each team will get one or two business advisors. I was invited to Walton High school as a business advisor for a group that was designing recyclable bags for shopping. So it was quite appropriate to have me representing the retail business. Other projects included bags and wallets made out of recycled crisp bags! And a clock made out of old records (LPs), Mouse mats, and many more.

But my relationship with the school started a couple of month before that, when I was invited to do a talk on their careers day at the school. The careers day is a big annual event at Walton High School, were students can have an overview of various career paths, in a big exhibition usually attended by representatives of various local, national and international businesses. Local politicians were also present to talk about council and political careers. I was invited to represent ASDA Stores Ltd.

I had a power point presentation to give and then there was a Q&A session. It was interesting to see the pupils' faces when they realized how versatile career possibilities are at ASDA. I did in total four presentations to four different classes. In one younger class, one of the students asked me if I owned ASDA! Other questions included salary and promotions. One set of girls were impressed by the possibility of a fashion career at George (ASDA's clothing brand).

Anyway, back to the Young Enterprise Project. My team was designing re-usable bags made out of sustainable materials. Their idea was to create a new design to draw on the bag to make it more appealing. They were mainly straw bags. I suggested to have customised designs which would set them apart from the bags you can buy at any supermarket.

So work began, I asked them to prepare a set of designs, like a catalogue, from which shoppers can choose, and the bags will be made in front of the buyers at the stall (they had to sell the bags at a local market stall). In my opinion, this would make the bags more authentic, and create a spectacle by which they can attract the attention of prospective shoppers. It will also make their stall more exciting. ASDA donated the blank bags for them to use.

We had several meetings (usually on Wednesdays) and finally we had almost 100 bags ready to sell, plus more to be designed on the day. The project was very successful and they even came to ASDA to show and sell their bags after.

This project worked quite well for ASDA, promoting our recycling initiatives and encourages shoppers to use less plastic bags. It also showed our involvement with schools and careers.

Since 2008, I was involved with a local charity, called the Friends of Staffordshire Young Musicians (FOSYM). They support promising local musicians, and run music programmes in schools as well as co-organizing the Stafford Music festival.

In 2009 I became the Treasurer of the charity, and managed to secure a grant from the ASDA Foundation to develop a website for the charity. It was my idea that the charity needs a website to connect with young people, and being a member of the Committee I pushed it through and the Committee members agreed. I also designed the charity's website myself (I have a background in web design, as I worked in a Software design house after finishing my University).

One unusual project we took part in, was the Katyn memorial in Cannock chase.

In 1940, in a tragic massacre near Katyn, almost all Polish elite officers and government officials were murdered in suspicious circumstances in Russia.

In 2010, the sad tragedy was repeated and the Polish president along with most of the government ministers died in a plane crash over Russian soil. History repeating itself? exactly 70 years after the first massacre.

The Polish community in Stafford has decided to build a new memorial in Stafford near Cannock chase to remember all those who died in the first and second tragic massacres.

The polish community in Stafford is over 1000 strong, and many of them settled just after WW2 when they came fleeing Nazi Germany. Many have memories of Stafford over 50 years ago. The Polish White Eagle club is in the centre of the community, offering functions, dances, children activates and language lessons, to maintain the polish traditions. It is a great venue that is used by other charities as well.

The club approached me for funding for its community project to build the memorial, and we have put an application forward. We have worked on this for a few months, and the application was successful and we got £900!

It is important to remember the past, learn from it, and make sure these tragedies never happen again. This is the only memorial of its kind in the UK.

The official grant presentation ceremony took place at the Polish Club (White Eagle) in Riverway, Stafford, on May 27th 2010. The Chairman of the Polish Ex-Combatants Association in Stafford, Mr. Edward Herus, attended along with Mr. Marian Nowakowsky, the Secretary of the Polish Club in Stafford.

I guess it is now clear how versatile my job was, and how varied was the spectrum of good causes and events that we supported. It is fair to say that we successfully supported or were involved in organizing every major charity and community event between 2005 and 2010. Whether it is to do with kids, young people, elderly, disabled or even memories of people who passed away, as long as it had an impact on the local community and would benefit local people in one way or another, we were supporting it.

Needless to say that the sad part of my job, in some cases is to turn people down when they request support or sponsorship. I had many funding request letters on my desk every week asking for donations; from a small raffle prize for a church fete, to sponsorship of a rugby team, to fruits for an open day at a school, etc. Unfortunately, due to the large number of requests and the limited budget we had to turn many down. We had to have a criteria to select who we support. It is impossible to help everyone, as much as I would've loved to.

The criteria I always used had three factors. First, how big an impact an event will have on the local community. How many people will be affected or will benefit from it. If it is a small group, with a very specialized event that will only benefit those who take part, then it is not favourable.

The second factor is how much of an impact would our support make. Sometimes a little amount can go a long way. In other occasions, my knowledge and experience in PR, or simply knowing the right people would help the charity event much more than money or donations. In general, my view was (and still is), that for a large company like ASDA to get involved and use our resources to support an event properly we need to be the main sponsor one way or another.

This also leads to the final factor: how much PR coverage are we likely to get as a result. This is not being heartless, but in business we always have to look at the return on investment (ROI). The more potential a story has for PR, the more resources we can put into it and turn it into success. I can also then justify the expenses to my superiors in the HQ in Leeds.

I tried to help as many causes as I possibly could, and sometimes overstretched myself, but I really enjoyed making a difference locally. I felt ASDA was a pedestal, from which I could serve the local community. And in fairness to ASDA, they gave me the freedom to do so, and trusted me. I guess it is also due to the fact that the role was new and still being shaped, which gave me the opportunity to tweak it and change it as I needed to.

Clock wise, top: Carrier bag recycling event,2008. No Vat on juices petition, with Stafford MP David Kidney, 2007, the opening of the Marshlands Special School Sensory Garden, 2006, and the Walton Village children's Playground £10,000 grant, 2008.

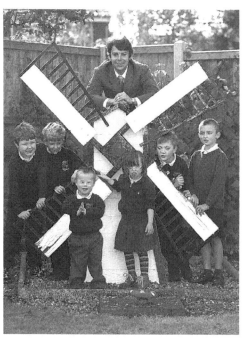

Chapter Seven

Local, National and Global

As a company, ASDA supported a few national high profile charities, for which we raised millions of pounds every year. These were like Tickled Pink, Breast Cancer Research, which ASDA supported for over 13 years and raised over £20 million in the process, BBC Children In Need, for which over £1 million is raised annually by ASDA.

There were are Tommy's Children appeal and Every Man Cancer charity. Not to mention our own Pedal Power this started in 2009 with a successful £1 million raised in the first year.

But there were also tens and hundreds of smaller local and national charities, that we supported in our local regions. These were chosen by people like me, and every year we supported a major one, and many smaller local charities that really benefit the local community. Our support included sponsorship, store collections, PR and marketing as well as spreading awareness and raising charities' profiles.

This is may come as a surprise to the reader, but a couple of volunteers standing with a collection bucket in the Foyer of an average ASDA store could raise up to £1000 per day. This is simply due to the large footfall figures: on a typical Saturday, between 8000 and 12000 shoppers pass through the doors. It is simple mathematics.

But what is more important, is a remark made by one of our store's GSM's, Kev Prince, in a discussion we had about charity collections and their effectiveness. He said that shoppers come to a supermarket ready to spend. This couldn't be more true in my opinion. People don't come to ASDA to browse. They are here because they need to buy this or that, food or other household products. So they are in the right set of mind for spending. They also usually have change after they shopping. And finally, they are psychologically more relaxed having done the huge task of a weekly shop (not something most people enjoy, as they have to do it! I don't!). All that makes people more perceptive and willing to give on the way out.

That makes a charity collection in a supermarket much more effective than in any other place, and that is why I was inundated with letters and requests for collections and bag packing. I remember in one of the St. John Ambulance annual Pre-conference lunch, to which I was invited to by the commander of St. John Ambulance, Mrs. Maureen Hopton, as a sponsor, the speaker who was also the Fundraising manager of ST. John in Stafford, and a good friend of mine, Amanda Donnells-Smith said that supermarket collections are one of the major income sources for St. John Ambulance. St. John Ambulance in Staffordshire raise over £20,000 annually this way.

It was difficult to find the balance to support a variety of causes. There are always advantages and disadvantages for supporting national and local charities.

National or big charities have a great advantage: people know them. It is much easier to get people to donate if they know what it is for, and know the charity. We never had problems with Breast Cancer research, BBC Children In Need, or major charities. On the other hand, people get frustrated as the money goes national, and no one can tell where it will end up.

Local charities have the advantage that the public can see where the funds are going, and it is usually a local cause on their doorstep. The disadvantage is, however, that many people don't know enough about them, as they don't get enough media coverage. That is certainly the feedback that I had from shoppers.

So, I used to divide my diary evenly between local and national causes, and I felt that local charities needed more and benefited more from the exposure. So I always supported them, and prepared their press releases and made sure they get good coverage on the day. I felt the local papers were doing the same and focusing on local issues, which is what matters to local people.

I used the word "local community", "local girl or boy", "local cause" a lot in my press releases and tried to put events into a local context. This increased the coverage we had from the local papers and increased the interest from the public in what we do. My aim was to turn their shopping trip into an informative one, and not just ask them for donations, but give them some information as well (my 3G rule!). This worked very well for us and for the local charities, which were desperate for funds and were being squeezed out by larger national charities.

Local

Many of the causes we supported locally started out as a collection or donation request letters in my pigeon hole. I turned them onto events and festivals whenever I could, to maximize the impact for them in terms of funds and exposure and for us in terms of PR.

I always felt that this was my strength: turning a boring collection or fundraiser into a fully fledged event. Many of the smaller charities don't have marketing or PR positions and rely totally on volunteers, who do a great job but don't have the PR sense needed for a bigger impact especially at a venue like ASDA. I did my best to help them, write their press releases, invite the needed guests, like the Mayor or MP. I also set up the photo shoots and prepared the programmes for the day.

With every event we had, I lend myself to the charity or organization and become their own PR officer. I spent hours learning about their history, interesting facts and more information to make the press release into an interesting story that the papers would be interested in. I had to see it from their perspective. I made sure the event was not about ASDA.

This way, the public and the newspaper editors will not get fed up! This was indirect marketing, and it is much more powerful than an ad in the paper in some cases. Its impact lasts much longer too. I was trying to influence the public perception in favour of ASDA.

Among the many local causes we supported was Katherine House Hospice (KHH). It is a local residential and day care home for the terminally ill. It relies on donations to run, and requires over £2 million per annum to survive. It is a very local cause, and the Hospice is located on the grounds of the Stafford General Hospital.

My relationship with KHH started in 2006, when one of their Event Fundraisers, James Lunney, who had just joined them, contacted me about sponsoring a new charity fundraiser they were about to launch: the Women's Midnight Walk. Four years later, every September, hundreds of Women in Stafford embark on a 6 mile walk to raise money for KHH. It started as a small walk, with 300 women, and now has in excess of 1000 every year. We supplied the refreshments and promoted the tickets sale and banners.

Since 2006, we supported the charity in many of its fundraisers. For example we helped them promote their Christmas Snowball lottery, and sell the tickets in the ASDA foyer. We launched it one year at ASDA, dressed up in Elf's and Santa's and got a front page story in the Express and Star.

Another local charity we worked with was the People First Disabled Society. It organizes weekly meetings and Bingo nights for disabled people in Stafford, with various disabilities. It also organizes day trips to the sea side and theatre. It relies totally on donations and volunteers.

I met with the Chairman of the charity Alison for the first time in 2006, and we have worked together on several events. Our first successful event was organizing a Christmas party for the members in 2006. I dressed up as Santa, and we booked a function room at the Tillington Hall Hotel in Stafford (I know the Marketing Manager and we got a huge discount, also it being a charity). We invited the Mayor of Stafford, at that time, Cllr Brian Price. We donated the presents, and I went around and gave the members their presents. We had about 50 people.

In summer 2007, we organized a big fundraiser for the same charity, and theme was Country and Western. We contacted some fans we knew, and they came in to the ASDA Foyer dressed up in authentic Cowboy costumes, even the ladies. We had eight people in total, and we had all the decorations including the flags. We really turned the Foyer into a Western Saloon! We raised over £800 and everyone had great fun. I dressed up myself, and we had three news paper articles.

In 2008, we worked with the Staffordshire Blind, a local charity that supports people with sight problems, and has over 500 members in the Stafford area. We had the guide dogs in the Foyer of ASDA, and raised over £400 in one day.

We also raised awareness of the charity as many people didn't know what they do or that they even existed, despite the Head Quarters being a mere 10 minute walk from the town centre. We also got an article in the paper with the Charities contacts. In my opinion, that was more important than the actual amount raised.

We also held fundraisers with the Donna Louise Children's Trust, a charity that provides day care and advice for children who are terminally ill, and is based only eight miles out of Stafford. One of the Patrons of the charity is Robbie Williams, the singer and Lord Stafford.

Every Christmas we had a hospital round, where I dressed up as an Elf and had a Santa with me, and we went around the Stafford Hospital, giving elderly patients gifts for Christmas. It was a joint project between us and the Stafford Hospital League of Friends. We also did the same for children.

105

Apart from local charities, we also supported local clubs and youth groups. At Christmas time, we let Air cadets; Sea cadets and Army cadets come into the store and help customers pack their bags for donations. We usually had about 10 youngsters on ten checkouts and they used to move around depending on how busy the tills are.

I was also keen to work closely with the Stafford Borough Council on various initiatives, such as the NHS Stop smoking campaign, promoting and raising awareness of the council's Fostering and Adoption schemes (they had a huge yellow bus called Reggie, the adoption bus, and they held surgeries in the car park). We even helped in the Council local elections, by having a ballot box for the public feedback at ASDA. We had the Council cycling unit in store several times to promote cycling and give advice on cycling routes and maps around the area.

We worked with the council and walking club to promote exercise and power walking, and they even choose ASDA as start location for their walks. We also sponsored them with fruit and water for the walkers.

When ASDA Stafford got planning permission to build a new mezzanine level in 2007, I invited the local council, local newspaper editors and the local MP David Kidney to an unveiling ceremony at ASDA. I set up a display in the Foyer (entrance area of the store), and built a scale model of the proposed design and had it displayed for guests and the public.

We also worked closely with the Police on various events and awareness days. For example we had one event were the police raised awareness of bike theft, and we had two police officers in the Foyer marking shoppers bikes for free and explaining the best ways to protect the bikes.

I guess it the convenient location and the number of people that pass through the doors everyday is what makes ASDA such a great venue. We also have free parking and we are only 10 minute walk from the town centre. All that makes it a very attractive venue for all sorts of events.

National

As I mentioned before, ASDA supports several corporate charities every year, such as Tickled Pink and Children In Need.

But we also had our own charity, Pedal Power, and we have organizing various fundraisers in store for it. Sometimes, I got the local council cycling unit involved with us, to give the public information and not just asking for money for nothing.

One fundraiser was a 100 mile exercise bike ride in the Foyer, in which department managers took turns to complete the challenge. Another challenge was a 24 hour Bedathon. We set up a double bed at the front of the store, and we had two managers in there all the time for 24 hours!

For Tickled Pink, as I already mentioned, we had Rock'n'Roll days, Grease, and Pink Cadillacs! But we also had less glamorous fundraisers. I organized a tyre wash and dressing, were by for £1 donation, we would wash your car tyres and dress them up with a special spray to keep them clean and back. It also protects them. Cars being my hobby, I knew what to do. I got the equipment and the sprays for free from Halfords, who kindly supported us in the fundraiser. I even invited the Mayor of Stafford, at that time, Cllr Jean Taberner, and cleaned the Mayoral car tyres to launch the event!

We also held a few car wash events, in the back car park.

One interesting fundraiser we had started off a bit normal. It was a fundraiser for the RNLI (Royal National Lifeboat Institute). We had the usual displays in the Foyer, I asked the fundraisers to wear their life jackets and it was going well.

Then, from chatting to the volunteers, I found out then two of them just got married! That is a great story, but what's even better, they were both over 80 years old! Now that is a super story! So, straight away, I presented them with flowers, announced it to everyone in store, and got a great photo. I sent the story to the papers and we got a good piece of PR.

In Christmas 2007 and 2008 we also had the British Red Cross Volunteers, who were university students from around the region. They bag packed, and were all dressed up in red tops, Christmas hats and red tights! It looked great!

One charity, which was close to my heart and to ASDA location wise, was St. John Ambulance. I first came across it in 2006, and ever since we had a very special relationship, which benefited both of us (by that I mean ASDA and St. John). I personally had great admiration for what they do, relying on volunteers, saving lives and even covering for the ambulance service itself. I have also seen how dedicated everyone is, and how well organized they are.

I had great respect for the work they do, and personally knew their Commander in their Staffordshire National HQ, in Stafford, Dame Maureen Upton. She is lovely lady who is loved and admired by everyone. The charity itself goes back over 150 years, with origins from the crusades over 800 years ago. They still operate the Eye Hospital in Jerusalem. Their Patron is HRH the Duke of York. Its history is really fascinating, and I was given a book about it by Maureen, which I found very interesting.

We organized many fundraisers and First Aid awareness days at ASDA through the years, which would be too much to mention. We even had an Ambulance van at the entrance of the store, open for the public too look inside. We had CPR demonstrations in the Foyer. We even held a Tea Cosy party in our customer restaurant for the ladies of St. John. We organized many interesting events.

One project in particular though, we started together and it continued to this day very successfully. In 2008, St. John Ambulance approached me for anew ambitious project they had. It was the Ambulance Bicycles. These were specially prepared heavy duty all-terrain bikes that had all the basic equipment you would have in an ambulance, only in miniature form. This would be very useful in crowded locations (such as the V Music Festival, open air situation with crowds, or simply in towns to reduce emissions and working in the town and city centres).

I was really amazed by the idea from the start and felt it would be an instant success. I also saw the PR potential in the story. It is something new and it will be a hit. It also sends a good environmental message, and it was in line with our Pedal Power charity. It was one of those win-win situations.

So I applied for funding for the project over the years, and we secured thousands of pounds for it to get off the grounds. Each bike with equipment costs over £2000. Today, in Stafford, there are six fully equipped St. John Ambulance bikes with trained riders. They are being deployed every week in various events.

In 2007, we launched an appeal to reduce VAT (Value Added Tax) on fresh juices and smoothies. As it was, these drinks were considered luxury, and were subject to 17.5% VAT. So we launched a petition, and asked our customers to sign it. If we got enough signatures, we would then take it to Downing Street.

I contacted Stafford MP, Mr. David Kidney and he supported us and attended the launch. He then delivered the petition to Downing Street on our behalf. This was a good PR campaign that really got the public involved, and at the same time promoted healthy eating and ASDA's juices (we sampled them for free in the Foyer).

Global

As a multinational corporation, and a responsible retailer, ASDA supported various global initiatives, that had an impact on the business and that were of importance to our customer base.

A good example of that is the environment. We had a major drive from the company to encourage recycling and reduce carrier bag usage. This was also motivated by the government and the various pressure groups that attacked supermarkets in the UK for excessive use of plastics in packaging and carrier bags. But because of the difficulty of cutting down on packaging, supermarkets deviated their focus onto carrier bag. Supermarkets launched massive campaigns to encourage the recycling of carrier bags. To be fair, though, carrier bags only represent a small fraction of the actual packaging waste on the shelves. But it is a good start.

We organized many events in conjunction with my contacts in the local Council, to encourage carrier bag recycling and give the public more information and advice. When the new colour coded bins were introduced in homes, we held an awareness week to tell the public about it. We also had a full recycling station in the car park, for glass, plastic and even clothing (we worked with a company called European Textile Recycling (ETR) who collected the containers and sold the clothes to Europe, then donated a percentage to our charities).

In one recycling event, we launched our new Bags for Life initiative. Shoppers can buy a green bag, made out of recycled material, for 5 pence. If the bag breaks or splits, they can bring it back and get a new one for free. To promote the scheme, I organized an event in the foyer and wore a suit I made out of the bags to attract people's attention, complete with a hat! The story made the front page!!

Another aspect we pushed in ASDA, was global warming. We had a campaign in 2008 to encourage shoppers to buy local produce. We had a complete aisle of local products, produced with 20 miles of the store. This sent the right environmental message, but at the same time improved ASDA's image (against allegations of monopoly and squeezing local farmers). The campaign later lost momentum, and customers themselves preferred the brands they were used to. I invited several local farmers (our suppliers) to the store on various occasions to talk to customers to promote the campaign.

That was a very brief overview of some of the causes and initiatives we supported in ASDA, and some of the events we held over the years.

Top: Western Fundraiser. The Ambulance Bikes project.
Left: with Dame Maureen Upton, St. John Ambulance Commander.
Below: Army fundraiser, 2008.
With Tim Atkin, the BBC wine expert during filming in-store for BBC Saturday kitchen, 2010.

Clockwise, Top: Children in Need fundraiser at ASDA, World Cup 2010 promotion, RNLI fundraiser , PDSA 100 pet toys donation as part of the pet week, and a donation to the Midlands Air Ambulance at the launch of their annual lottery appeal at ASDA Stafford.

Above: I organized the Save Our School campaign at Marshlands Special School, where I was a governor to fight the severe budget cuts between 2008 and 2010.   It worked.

Below: new Mums goody bags donation At Stafford Hospital.
The new Wii games room at Silkmore Children's Centre. (bottom).

Chapter Eight

Names and Faces

Over the years, through my work and personal contacts, I met many interesting and famous people, from local celebrities, authorities, to national and international stars, and even royalty. I realized the importance of connections and networking for the PR business from day one. So I strived to attend as many functions and meeting as possible, to meet more and more people. My business card was my best friend. I had some in every jacket and suit I wore.

Through my involvement with the Rotary Club of Stafford Knot, and the local Council, as well as the media, I had the pleasure and the honour to meet so many people.

Through the events I organized as well as the social events I attended, my circle of acquaintances grew bigger and bigger. I was being invited to the elite events in the Stafford social life, attended by the crème de la crème of Stafford such as the Mayor's Ball, which takes place twice a year, in March and December.

The Mayor's Ball is a glamorous event, and though the proceeds all go for charity, it is an opportunity to dress up and meet the right people. Men usually wear their Tuxedos and ladies show off their posh frocks!

I was also invited to various Charity evenings, St. John Ambulance Conferences, Gala nights at the local Theatre, Political gatherings and events, the Mayor's parade, and the Mayor Making.

The Gala night at the Gatehouse theatre in June every year is a big event in the Stafford social calendar. Over the past few years, the Gatehouse produced a series of open air shows at the Stafford Castle. These were modern twists on Shakespeare's classics, such as Romeo and Juliet and the Twelfth Night.

A huge tent was set up under the castle, with wine and buffet for VIP guests, including the Mayor. The stage was set at the foot of the hill, and the castle was lit up behind the props in a magical spectacle.

The Mayor's making is another special occasion that takes place in May every year. That is the time when the current Mayor steps down and the new Mayor take office. It takes place in the County Buildings in Stafford, in Martin Street. I beautiful building, over 100 years old, and has a huge chamber that looks like the senate or the House of Commons, but circular. It also has a famous library, lined with oak and full of treasures and paintings. The entrance has a massive staircase covered with a red carpet over the marble steps. It looks like a movie set.

All local political party representatives, local councillors and dignitaries are invited to this annual event, as well as special guests and VIP's. It reminds me of a mini coronation for Stafford. The Mayor's Sergeant announces the proceedings and they follow a certain tradition. After that, everyone is invited to a buffet in the back room, or reception. I met most of the local Councillors at those events.

I have personally known fives Mayors of Stafford, in chronological order, Cllr Mike Shone, Cllr Brian Price, Cllr Ann Edgeller, Cllr Jean Taberner, and Cllr Malcolm Millichap.

I also know Deputy Mayor Cllr Brian Price and Cllr Ray Barron, both are good friends.

I have known Mr. David Kidney MP for many years, I know Mr. Jeremy Lefroy the current MP.

During the 2009 Local County Council elections, I helped a good friend of mine, Cllr Ray Barron in his campaign, by canvassing and leafleting, and he won a very difficult seat for the conservative party. I got involved with the party, and as a result, I met more people at the helm of the Conservative Party, including Mr. Eric Pickles, during his visit to Stafford for the annual Conservative Association of Stafford dinner, which I was invited to.

I have also known Mr. Charles Boote, the Chairman of the Campaign Committee of the Conservative party in the Stafford region and Mr. Amias Stafford North Cote, the Chairman of the Stafford Conservative Association.

I also knew Cllr. Mike Heenan, the Leader of the Stafford Borough Council, Mr. Ian Thompson, the Chief Executive of the Staffordshire County Council, Cllr. Terry Dix, the Chairman of the Staffordshire County Council and Cllr Philip Atkins, the Leader of the East Staffordshire Borough Council.

I have met on several occasions, Mr. James Howley, the Lord Lieutenant of Stafford, and the Queens representative, as well as the High Sherriff of Stafford, Richard Haszard.

I have known Mr. Steve McTigue, the Mayor's Sergeant.

Through our involvement in local sports, I met Mr. Steve Bull MBE, the Wolves football legend. I met Mr. Jon Downing, the Chairman of the Stafford Rangers FC, Mr. Stan Robinson, of the famous Haulage company and who is a prolific sponsor of the club, Mr. Brian Gayton, the Chairman of the Stafford Rugby Club, and several professional Cricketers through Kwick Cricket.

I met Eleanor Simmond OBE, the Paraolympic Gold medallist in the Stafford Charity Bicycle ride.

I met the Staffordshire Police Commissioner, head of the Cannock Chase Police.

I had the pleasure of meeting world class pianist and organist Jean Martyn, and Mr. Nigel Taylor, the famous conductor.

For my services to St. John Ambulance, Dame Maureen Upton, the Commander of St. John Ambulance in Staffordshire, invited me as a guest of St. John Ambulance to the opening ceremony of the new St. John memorial at the National Memorial Arboretum. I had the honour of meeting HRH the Duke of Gloucester, the Patron of St. John Ambulance.

On Sat. 19th June 2010, I was again invited as a guest of St. John Ambulance in Staffordshire and its Commander, Dame Maureen Upton to the annual Commemoration and Re-Dedication service of the most venerable Order of St. John, at St. Paul Cathedral in London. It was a magical event. Representatives of St. John Ambulance from all over the World were present, as well as the Grand priors and the Knights of the order, who paraded through the cathedral to the sounds of the organs, choir and fanfare. They were all dressed up in the official regalia of the order. Guests included the Lord Mayor of London, and the Sherriff, as well as dignitaries from all over the world. Attendance was by invitation only. The cathedral was closed to the public on that day.

In her charity's "Home Start" 25th Anniversary celebrations, I met the Dowager Countess of Harrowby, at her estate, Sandon Hall, near Stafford. I met the Grand Prior of St. John Ambulance in England and the Islands, and the commander of St. John Ambulance in Staffordshire.

I have also met the international wine master Tim Atkin, known for his BBC programmes.

I have also known Mrs Tony Brisby, the former Chief Executive of the Stafford Hospital, and Julie Bailey, the founder of the Cure the NHS Campaign, who protested against failing in the Stafford Hospital.

On the 22nd of June 2010, I had the greatest honour of all: In recognition for my work for the local community in Stafford, I was invited by Lord Chamberlain to the Queens Garden party, at Buckingham Palace. It was a magical and historical event.

Every year, her Majesty the Queen hosts three garden parties to recognize outstanding services to the British Empire, and to honour those people who stood out and served their local and national peers. Two parties are held at Buckingham Palace, and one in Scotland.

Guests include Royalty, Diplomats and various sections of the community. Nominees are put forward by the local authorities and the Lord Chamberlain then approves the list.

The invitation came in a sealed envelope, with the Royal seal, and gold writing. Various security checks were conducted and forms were filled.

It was a great honour to see her Majesty the Queen. We were lucky and stood only a few feet away from her, the Duke of Edinburgh and Prince Edward and his wife Sophie. It was a clear and hot summer day and everyone was dressed up.

I put on my morning coat (Black Tailcoat, and top hat), it took me some days to find the correct dress code, as it is very strict at the Palace. I booked first class train tickets (you need to arrive in style, this doesn't happen every day!) We arrived in London at 1:00pm, and were in the queue to enter the Palace at 2:00pm.

We went through the Grand Entrance of the Palace, beyond which the public are not allowed. We walked through the main foyer, the exact spot where British prime ministers arrive to meet the queen. We then walked through the Queens gallery, again, not open to the public. Finally, we reached the terrace, at 3:00pm, from which we walked to the Palace Gardens (again, not open to the general public).

The tea and refreshments were served at the tea tent, and guests could stroll through the gardens. At 4:00pm, the Queen and the Duke of Edinburgh came out to the terrace, and the National Anthem was played. She wore a primrose yellow dress and a matching hat, and the

Duke wore a grey morning coat. The Guards of Yeomen surrounded the lawn. The Queen then met some of the guests, presented to her by Lord Chamberlain, as she walked towards the Royal Tea Tent. The party finished at 6:00pm, and there was a huge queue for Taxi's afterwards, but everyone was very pleased. I am still excited now!

It was a magical experience and we met many famous politicians and celebrities there, but most of all, we were in the heart of the British Establishment, with its heritage and tradition. What a fantastic reward for all the hard work.

I have met so many people that it is hard to list or remember everyone, but I enjoy meeting people and being involved in and organizing various functions.   But most of all, I enjoy making a difference. It is only now when I stop I think about it, I realize how many faces and names I've seen and forgotten. But it is work and achievements that stay on and will be remembered.   That, I hope I have done.

Civic list! Mayor's Ball, campaigning with Cllr Ray Barron, in the 2009 local elections, celebrating Conservative Victory in 2009 with Charles Boote, Conservative Campaign Chairman in Staffordshire.

Mayor's Ball, 2009, with Stafford Mayor, Cllr Jean Taberner, and County Council Chief Exec. Ian Thompson.

CW, Top: At Buckingham Palace for the Queen's Garden Party in June 2010, with the High Sherriff of Staffordshire, with Rotary Club President, Stuart Cantrill, with TV presenter Suzi Perry, and with Real Estate Tycoon, Fred Pritchard at the annual Conservative dinner where I met Cabinet Minister Eric Pickles.

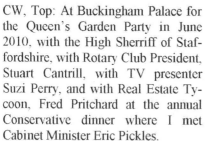

About the Author

Sherif E. Hegazy, was born on 30th April 1978. His father, El-Sayed is a University Professor and Marine Consultant. He is the inspiration behind many of Sherif's achievements.

At secondary school he won the International award *"The First Step to Nobel Prize in Physics"*, organized by the Polish Academy of Science, in 1994.

He went to University and studied Computer Engineering between 1995 and 2000, gaining a BSc degree with first class Honours. He went on to obtain an MSc in Computer Engineering.

Between 2002 and 2005 he lectured at the University and ran his own web design and Internet solutions business. He published 21 academic research papers.

He also successfully completed the Oracle Database certification programme (OCP, DBA) in 2003. He also has qualifications in web design, graphic design and animation.

While lecturing at University, he successfully supervised a team of students at the International RoboCon Robot design competition finals in Bangkok, Thailand, in 2003.

He joined ASDA Wal-Mart in 2005 as the Events and Marketing Coordinator, and was later the Head of local Community Programme in the Stafford area, UK, until 2012. He won three national Gold awards for PR and Community Involvement and several Gold awards for his Events. He was chosen to be one of the Faces of ASDA in the 2010 Christmas national Ads campaign.

Sherif speaks fluent English, Russian, Arabic and German. He also speaks some Italian and French.

His Hobbies include Classic cars (he was the Chairman of the Jaguar XJS Club, www.xjs.org.uk), Tennis, Sailing, Skiing, Dancing and photography.

Affiliations

The author is a member of the following societies and charities:

Rotary International.

St. John Ambulance.

Oddfellows Society.

Friends of Staffordshire's Young Musicians (FOSYM), Treasurer.

Board of Governors of Marshlands Special School, Stafford.

Board of Governors of Walton High School, Stafford.

The White Eagle Polish Club.

Jaguar XJS Club (Chairman).

Royal Yachting Association (RYA).

Blithfield Sailing Club, Staffordshire.

IET (Institute of Engineering and Technology).

The National Trust.

CEROC Dance clubs UK.

Contact Sherif on:

sherif_hegazy2000@yahoo.com

hegazy@ntlworld.com

Facebook:

Sherif Hegazy

References

ASDA Stores Ltd.   www.asda.com

British Heart Foundation   www.bhf.org.uk

British Red Cross   www.redcross.org.uk

Express & Star Newspapers   www.expressandstar.com

Friends of Staffordshire Young Musicians   www.fosym.org

Katherine House Hospice   www.khhospice.org.uk

Marshlands Special School   www.marshlands.staffs.sch.uk

Rotary International   www.rotary.org

Royal National Life Boat Institution   www.rnli.org.uk

St. John Ambulance   www.sja.org

Stafford Borough Council   www.staffordbc.gov.uk

Stafford Gatehouse Theatre   www.staffordgatehousetheatre.co.uk

Stafford Rangers FC   www.staffordrangersfc.co.uk

The Stafford Post Newspaper   www.icstafford.icnetwork.co.uk

The Staffordshire Newsletter   www.staffordshirenewsletter.co.uk

Oddfellows Society   www.oddfellows.co.uk

Wikipedia: The free Encyclopaedia   www.wikipedia.org

ASDA

1. ^ "Contact the right service team." Asda. Retrieved on 20 June 2010.
2. ^ "Global powers of retail report - wal mart remains world's largest global retailer - Deloitte & Touche". www.deloitte.com. http://www.deloitte.com/dtt/press_release/0,1014,cid%253D196099,00.html. Retrieved 2008-10-07.
3. ^ *a* *b* "Wal-Mart buys Asda in UK retail shock". Eurofood. 17 June 1999. http://findarticles.com/p/articles/mi_m0DQA/is_1999_June_17/ai_55041044. Retrieved 2008-04-06.
4. ^ "Co-op buys Somerfield for £1.57bn". *BBC News Online* (BBC). 2008-07-16. http://news.bbc.co.uk/1/hi/business/7508982.stm. Retrieved 2008-10-06.
5. ^ "1920 to 1960 - In the Beginning". *All About Asda*. Asda. 2005. http://www.about-asda.co.uk/inside-asda/our-history.asp. Retrieved 2008-10-09.
6. ^ Cinven - Case studies
7. ^ "ASDA/WAL-MART - A Corporate Profile". Corporate Watch. http://www.corporatewatch.org/?lid=800. Retrieved 2008-04-06.
8. ^ "Allan Leighton". Management Today. 25 August 2005. http://www.managementtoday.co.uk/search/article/492390/mt-interview-allan-leighton/. Retrieved 2008-04-05.
9. ^ Hope, Christopher; Hall, James (28 January 2008). "Wal-Mart did lobby Blair over Asda". London: *The Telegraph*. http://www.telegraph.co.uk/finance/newsbysector/retailandconsumer/2783372/Wal-Mart-did-lobby-Blair-over-Asda.html. Retrieved 2008-10-09.
10. ^ "Asda acquires 12 NI Safeway stores". Northern Ireland News. 2005-06-06. http://www.4ni.co.uk/northern_ireland_news.asp?id=41262. Retrieved 2008-04-06.
11. ^ "Asda eyes up the Republic: ThePost.ie". archives.tcm.ie. http://archives.tcm.ie/businesspost/2005/06/12/story5576.asp. Retrieved 2008-10-09.
12. ^ . http://www.belfasttelegraph.co.uk/breaking-news/ireland/business/dunnes-urged-to-clarify-rumours-of-asda-takeover-14033905.html.
13. ^ Tyler, Richard (8 Nov 2009). "Wal-Mart 'sells' Asda for £6.9bn in group restructuring". *telegraph.co.uk* (London: Telegraph Media Group Limited). http://www.telegraph.co.uk/finance/newsbysector/retailandconsumer/6527054/Wal-Mart-sells-Asda-for-6.9bn-in-group-restructuring.html. Retrieved 2009-11-11.
14. ^ "Asda posts flat profits and is 'sold' in internal Walmart deal". *Retail Week*. Emap Ltd. 9 November 2009. http://www.retail-week.com/city/trading-update/asda-posts-flat-profits-and-is-sold-in-internal-walmart-deal/5007872.article. Retrieved 2009-11-11.
15. ^ "Asda promotes Andy Clarke to chief executive - Telegraph". telegraph.co.uk. http://www.telegraph.co.uk/finance/newsbysector/retailandconsumer/7711304/Asda-promotes-Andy-Clarke-to-chief-executive.html. Retrieved 2010-05-11.
16. ^ "Asda 'Thank You' TV ad - 30 sec advert". www.tellyads.com. http://www.tellyads.com/show_movie.php?filename=TA2532&advertiser=ASDA. Retrieved 2008-10-09.
17. ^ Sweney, Mark (2009-03-18). "Asda brings back 'pocket tap' ads". London: guardian.co.uk. http://www.guardian.co.uk/media/2009/mar/18/asda-pocket-tap-adverts. Retrieved 2009-07-15.
18. ^ "Asda 'Something Big' TV ad - 20 sec advert". www.tellyads.com. http://www.tellyads.com/show_movie.php?filename=TA5261&advertiser=Asda. Retrieved 2008-10-09.
19. ^ "Asda 'Comparison' TV ad - 20 sec advert". www.tellyads.com. http://www.tellyads.com/show_movie.php?filename=TA5744&advertiser=Asda. Retrieved 2008-10-09.
20. ^ "Asda 'Christmas' TV ad - 40 sec advert". www.tellyads.com. http://tellyads.com/show_movie.php?filename=TA7819. Retrieved 2008-12-05.
21. ^ "The Grocer 33 2009: Asda still cheapest, but Morrisons wins on service and stock". www.thegrocer.co.uk. http://www.thegrocer.co.uk/articles.aspx?page=articles&ID=200634. Retrieved 2009-06-21.

22. ^ "Asda made to drop low price claim", *BBC*, 17 August 2005.
23. ^ "Clean Up Fashion; Asda Walmart". http://www.cleanupfashion.co.uk/companies/asda.php. Retrieved 2006-11-23.
24. ^ "Fashion Victims". *War on Want*. 2006-12-15. http://www.waronwant.org/campaigns/supermarkets/fashion-victims/inform/13593-fashion-victims. Retrieved 2009-02-18.
25. ^ "Fashion Victims II". *War on Want*. 2008-12-01. http://www.waronwant.org/campaigns/supermarkets/fashion-victims/inform/16360-fashion-victims-ii. Retrieved 2009-02-18.
26. ^ "Dismay at commitment to cheap food by ASDA". http://www.nfuonline.com/x16312.xml. Retrieved 2009-10-30.
27. ^ "£2 Valentine flowers poverty alert". *War on Want*. 2009-02-13. http://www.waronwant.org/news/press-releases/16464-p2-valentine-flowers-poverty-alert. Retrieved 2009-02-18.
28. ^ "Asda Kwik Cricket". EBC. http://www.ecb.co.uk/development/kids/kwik-cricket/. Retrieved 2008-06-30.
29. ^ "Superbrands case studies: George". Brand Republic. 2006-04-18. http://www.brandrepublic.com/bulletins/design/article/554301/superbrand-case-studies-george/. Retrieved 2008-06-30.
30. ^ Mintel Clothing Retailing - UK, July 2005
31. ^ Supermarket unveils £60 wedding dress *Telegraph.co.uk*. Retrieved 6 October 2006.[dead link]
32. ^ Asda takes aim at Tesco with new stores,.
33. ^ "Asda to take over Netto stores in UK". BBC News. 2010-05-27. http://news.bbc.co.uk/1/hi/business/10171193.stm. Retrieved 2010-05-27.
34. ^ Finch, Julia (2006-12-05). "Asda's new stores prove not-so-Essential in the discount market". London: The Guardian. http://www.guardian.co.uk/business/2006/dec/05/supermarkets.asda. Retrieved 2008-10-09.
35. ^ "Asda Essentials trial continues despite store closure". IGD Retail Analysis. 2007-01-09. http://www.igd.com/analysis/news/index.asp?nid=3468. Retrieved 2007-01-11.
36. ^ "Asda Careers: Locations: Distribution". Asda. http://www.asda.jobs/all-about/locations/distribution_locations.html. Retrieved 2008-10-07.
37. ^ "Wal-Mart Stores, Inc. - Wal-Mart Announces The Sale Of Gazeley Limited Group". walmartstores.com. http://walmartstores.com/FactsNews/NewsRoom/8374.aspx. Retrieved 2008-10-07.
38. ^ Butler, Sarah; Seib, Christine (20 September 2006). "Asda ends Scottish Widows tie-up". London: The Times Online. http://business.timesonline.co.uk/tol/business/industry_sectors/retailing/article644642.ece. Retrieved 2008-10-09.
39. ^ "FAQs - About Asda". Asda. http://www.about-asda.com/faq/. Retrieved 2008-10-07.
40. ^ "ASDA Reward Credit Card Benefits". Asda. http://www.asdafinance.com/credit-cards-loans/credit-card/benefits/. Retrieved 2009-09-25.
41. ^ "TNS Worldpanel Grocers Share of Trade". *Great Britain Consumer Spend - 12 Week Summary to 22 March 2009*. Taylor Nelson Sofres plc. 2009. http://www.tnsglobal.com/news/news-0686D44B3AF84B6DB2B75A7CFA9ECFFA.aspx. Retrieved 2007-09-06.
42. ^ "Tesco 'top' in more parts of the UK". *BBC News Online* (BBC). 11 October 2006. http://news.bbc.co.uk/1/hi/business/6040552.stm. Retrieved 2008-05-22.
43. ^ . http://appointments.timesonline.co.uk/Sites/top_100_2005_and_sme/asda/.
44. ^ "Working for Asda". Asda. http://www.about-asda.com/inside-asda/working-for-asda.asp#rewards. Retrieved 2008-10-09.
45. ^ Clement, Barrie (14 December 2005). "Asda managers told Asian staff to show passports". London: The Independent. http://www.independent.co.uk/news/uk/this-britain/asda-managers-told-asian-staff-to-show-passports-519405.html. Retrieved 2008-10-09.
46. ^ "Asda Wal-Mart guilty of anti-trade union activity". *Food & Drink Europe.com*. 14 February 2006. http://www.foodanddrinkeurope.com/Retail/Asda-Wal-Mart-guilty-of-anti-trade-union-activity. Retrieved 2008-10-09.
47. ^ "Five-day strike by Asda workers". *BBC News Online* (BBC). 22 June 2006. http://news.bbc.co.uk/1/hi/business/5107156.stm. Retrieved 2008-10-09.

48. ^ "Asda industrial action called off". *BBC News Online* (BBC). 29 June 2006. http://news.bbc.co.uk/1/hi/business/5128260.stm. Retrieved 2008-10-09.
49. ^ "Dairy Price Fixing Firms Fined Millions". *Sky News*. 2007-12-07. http://news.sky.com/skynews/Home/Business/Asda-and-Sainsburys-Fined-Over-Dairy-Price-Fixing/Article/20071211296071?lid=ARTICLE_1296071_Asda%20and%20Sainsbury's%20Fined%20Over%20Dairy%20Price%20Fixing&lpos=Business_0. Retrieved 2008-10-09.
50. ^ "Asda Named Britain's Most Innovative Employer". www.asda.com. http://www.asda-press.co.uk/pressrelease/292. Retrieved 2009-03-25.

WALMART

1. ^ http://walmartstores.com/FactsNews/NewsRoom/9663.aspxhttp://walmartstores.com/FactsNews/NewsRoom/9663.aspx
2. ^ *a b* "Wal-Mart Stores, Inc. (Public, NYSE:WMT)." *Yahoo! Finance.* Retrieved on January 7, 2009.
3. ^ *a b c* Wal-Mart 2009 Annual Report, pg 30 (32)
4. ^ "Wal-Mart Stores, Inc. (Public, NYSE:WMT)." *Google Finance.* Retrieved on December 9, *2007.*
5. ^ *a b* Biesada, Alex. "Walmart Stores, Inc." *Hoover's.* Retrieved on October 13, 2006.
6. ^ Forbes Global 2000. Retrieved on June 6, 2010.
7. ^ "Contact Us." Wal-Mart. Retrieved on June 28, 2010.
8. ^ "Wal-Mart Quick Facts." United Food and Commercial Workers International Union. Retrieved on June 28, 2010.
9. ^ Ann Zimmerman (2010-06-07). "Rival Chains Secretly Fund Opposition to Wal-Mart". The Wall Street Journal. http://online.wsj.com/article/SB10001424052748704875604575280414218878150.html?. Retrieved 2010-06-08.
10. ^ Walton, Sam; Huey, John. *Sam Walton: Made in America: My Story.* New York: Bantam, 1993. ISBN 0-553-56283-5.
11. ^ http://hbswk.hbs.edu/item/2375.html
12. ^ Frank, T.A. "A Brief History of Wal-Mart." *The Washington Monthly.* April 1, 2006. Retrieved on July 24, 2006.
13. ^ *a b* "The Rise of Wal-Mart". *Frontline: Is Wal-Mart Good for America?.* 2004-11-16. http://www.pbs.org/wgbh/pages/frontline/shows/walmart/transform/cron.html. Retrieved 2007-09-19.
14. ^ *a b c* "The Wal-Mart Timeline." *Wal-Mart* (published on walmartfacts.com). Retrieved on July 24, 2006.
15. ^ Ranade, Sudhanshu. "Satellite Adds Speed to Wal-Mart." *The Hindu Business Line.* July 17, 2005. Retrieved on July 24, 2006].
16. ^ Longo, Donald. "Wal-Mart Hands CEO Crown to Glass - David Glass." *Discount Store News.* February 15, 1988. Retrieved on April 1, 2008.
17. ^ Staff Writer. "Wal-Mart Tests Similar Hypermarkets - Hypermart USA, Wal-Mart SuperCenter." *Discount Store News.* March 28, 1988. Retrieved on April 19, 2007.
18. ^ Byrnes, Nanette; Eidam, Michael. "Toys 'R' Us: Beaten at Its Own Game." *BusinessWeek.* March 29, 2004. Retrieved on July 25, 2006.
19. ^ Buerkle, Tom. "$10 Billion Gamble in U.K. Doubles Its International Business: Wal-Mart Takes Big Leap into Europe." *International Herald Tribune.* June 15, 1999. Retrieved on April 19, 2007.
20. ^ "Neighborhood Markets." *Wal-Mart* (website). Retrieved on April 19, 2007.
21. ^ Ortiz, John. "Can Kroger Slow Wal-Mart?" *Deseret Morning News.* October 26, 2005. Retrieved on July 25, 2006.
22. ^ "2000 Annual Report: Net Sales." *Wal-Mart.* Retrieved on April 19, 2007.
23. ^ *a b* Staff Writer. "Fortune 500." *CNN/Fortune.* April 16, 2007. Retrieved on July 15, 2007.
24. ^ Staff Writer. "Fortune 500." *CNN/Fortune.* April 17, 2006. Retrieved on July 15, 2007.

25. ^ Zook, Matthew; Graham, Mark (2006). "Wal-Mart Nation: Mapping the Reach of a Retail Colossus". in Brunn, Stanley D.. *Wal-Mart World: The World's Biggest Corporation in the Global Economy*. Routledge. pp. 15–25. ISBN 0-415-95137-2.

26. ^ *a b c d* Stone, Kenneth E. (1997). "Impact of the Wal-Mart Phenomenon on Rural Communities". (Published in *Proceedings: Increased Understanding of Public Problems and Policies - 1997*. Chicago, Illinois: Farm Foundation). *Iowa State University*. Retrieved on August 4, 2006.

27. ^ *a b* Stone, Kenneth E.; Georgeanne Artz, Albert Myles (2003). "The Economic Impact of Wal-Mart Supercenters on Existing Businesses in Mississippi". *Mississippi State University*. Retrieved on August 4, 2006.

28. ^ Barbaro, Michael; Gillis, Justin (September 6, 2005). "Wal-Mart at Forefront of Hurricane Relief". The Washington Post. http://www.washingtonpost.com/wp-dyn/content/article/2005/09/05/AR2005090501598.html. Retrieved 2009-03-10.

29. ^ Huffman, Mark (April 2, 2008). "Real Katrina hero? Wal-Mart, study says". MSN. http://articles.moneycentral.msn.com/Insurance/InsureYourHome/RealKatrinaHeroWalMartStudySays.aspx. Retrieved 2009-03-10.

30. ^ Bhatnagar, Parija (September 9, 2005). "Wal-Mart redeems itself, but what's next". CNN. http://money.cnn.com/2005/09/09/news/fortune500/walmart_image/index.htm. Retrieved 2009-03-10.

31. ^ Staff Writer. "Is Wal-Mart Going Green?" *MSNBC*. October 25, 2005. Retrieved on November 8, 2007.

32. ^ Berner, Robert. "Can Wal-Mart Wear a White Hat?" *BusinessWeek*. September 22, 2005. Retrieved on July 24, 2006.

33. ^ *a b* Gunther, Mark. "Wal-Mart sees green." *CNN*. July 27, 2006. Retrieved on November 8, 2007.

34. ^ Souder, Elizabeth. "Will Wal-Mart Sell Electricity One Day?." *RedOrbit*. January 28, 2007. Retrieved on March 31, 2008.

35. ^ Koenig, David. "Wal-Mart Targeting Upscale Shoppers." *ABC News*. March 22, 2006.

36. ^ Staff Writer. "Wal-Mart turns attention to upscale shoppers." *MSNBC*. March 23, 2006. Retrieved on December 1, 2007.

37. ^ Staff Writer. "Wal-Mart Rolling out New Company Slogan." *Reuters* via *The New York Times*. September 12, 2007. Retrieved on September 26, 2007.

38. ^ Armin (30 June 2008). "Less Hyphen, More Burst for Walmart". *Brand New*. UnderConsideration LLC. http://www.underconsideration.com/brandnew/archives/less_hyphen_more_burst_for_wal.php. Retrieved 9 August 2010.

39. ^ Jana, Reena (July 2, 2008). "Wal-Mart Gets a Facelift". BusinessWeek. http://www.businessweek.com/innovate/content/jul2008/id2008072_324653.htm?chan=top+news_top+news+index_news+%2B+analysis. Retrieved 2008-07-07.

40. ^ Talley, Karen (March 20, 2009). "UPDATE: Wal-Mart Giving US Employees $2B In Yearly Award Pgm". The Wall Street Journal. http://online.wsj.com/article/BT-CO-20090319-713086.html?mod=. Retrieved 2009-03-20.

41. ^ [1]

42. ^ Wal-Mart Re-Enters Digital Downloading of Movies With Purchase of Vudu - The Wall Street Journal - February 22, 2010

43. ^ *a b c d e f g h* "Wal-Mart 2006 Annual ReportPDF (1.91 MB)." *Wal-Mart*. 2006. Retrieved on July 26, 2006.

44. ^ Silberner, Joanne (September 21, 2006). "Wal-Mart to Sell Generic Drugs for $4". All Things Considered (National Public Radio). http://www.npr.org/templates/story/story.php?storyId=6119292. Retrieved 2009-03-10.

45. ^ Business Standard, Pharma Firms boost walmart revenues, 16 June 2008

46. ^ Staff Writer. "Wal-Mart Launches Online Movie Download Service." *Fox News*. February 6, 2007. Retrieved on February 14, 2007.

47. ^ Matt Richtel and Brad Stone. "Wal-Mart's Movie Download Service Passes into Ignominy." "International Herald Tribune". January 1, 2008. Retrieved on January 2, 2008.

48. ^ *a b c* Longo, Don. "Gasoline a Logical Extension of Wal-Mart's Reach." *Convenience Store News*. November 1, 2007. Retrieved on November 1, 2007.

49. ^ Wal-Mart shuttering 7-year old Bud's chain - Bud's Discount City | Discount Store News | Find Articles at BNET.com
50. ^ *a b c d* "Corporate Profile." *Wal-Mart*. Retrieved on December 7, 2009.
51. ^ "Albany.com: Largest Wal-Mart Supercenter In US Finds Home In Albany NY" Retrieved on December 23, 2008.
52. ^ "Wal-Mart woos Hispanics with new Supermercado." *Reuters*. Retrieved on December 20, 2009.
53. ^ "New Supermercado de Walmart Opens in Houston." Wal-Mart. April 28, 2009. Retrieved on June 28, 2010.
54. ^ Wollam, Allison. "Wal-Mart chooses Houston as test market for Supermercado de Walmart." *Houston Business Journal*. Friday March 20, 2009. Retrieved on June 28, 2010.
55. ^ Serrano, Shea. "Houston Soon to Have Supermercado de Walmart." *About.com*. Monday March 23, 2009. Retrieved on June 28, 2010.
56. ^ Moreno, Jenalia. "Wal-Mart gives its Supermercado concept a tryout." *Houston Chronicle*. April 30, 2009. Retrieved on June 29, 2010.
57. ^ *a b* "About Sam's Club." *www.samsclub.com*. Retrieved on November 1, 2007.
58. ^ Lohr, Steve (March 10, 2009). "Wal-Mart Plans to Market Digital Health Records System". The New York Times. http://www.nytimes.com/2009/03/11/business/11record.html?hp. Retrieved 2009-03-11.
59. ^ "2007 Annual Report." (PDF). *Wal-Mart*. Retrieved on November 1, 2007.
60. ^ "Sam's Club." *Wal-Mart*. Retrieved on December 7, 2009.
61. ^ "Wal-Mart International." *Wal-Mart*. Retrieved on June 4, 2010.
62. ^ Wal-Mart Corporate Fact SheetPDF." *Wal-Mart*. Retrieved on June 6, 2010.
63. ^ [2]. Retrieved July 22, 2010.
64. ^ "Wal-mart International UK. Retrieved on June 8, 2010.
65. ^ "Wal-Mart Reports Third Quarter Sales and Earnings." *Wal-Mart*. November 14, 2006. Retrieved on November 14, 2006.
66. ^ "Wal-Mart SEC Form 10-K." *U.S. Securities and Exchange Commission*. January 31, 2006. Retrieved on July 26, 2006.
67. ^ "Brazil Operations." *Wal-Mart*. June 2010. Retrieved on June 6, 2010.
68. ^ Norwegian Ministry of Finance (2006-06-06). "Two companies - Wal-Mart and Freeport - are being excluded from the Norwegian Government Pension Fund – Global's investment universe". http://www.regjeringen.no/en/dep/fin/Press-Center/Press-releases/2006/Two-companies---Wal-Mart-and-Freeport---.html?id=104396&epslanguage=EN-GB.
69. ^ *a b* The Ethical Council of the Government Pension Fund of Norway (15 November 2005). "Recommendation of 15 November 2005". The Ministry of Finance. http://www.regjeringen.no/en/dep/fin/Selected-topics/The-Government-Pension-Fund/Ethical-Guidelines-for-the-Government-Pension-Fund---Global-/Recommendations-and-Letters-from-the-Advisory-Council-on-Ethics/Recommendation-of-15-November-2005.html?id=450120.

Special thanks to Wikipedia, the Free Encyclopaedia, www.wikipedia.org

8801197R00074

Printed in Great Britain
by Amazon.co.uk, Ltd.,
Marston Gate.